I'M GLAD YOU ASKED!

Biblical Answers to Some of Life's Toughest Questions

BY

PASTOR ROD PARSLEY

Columbus, Ohio

U.S.A.

I'M GLAD YOU ASKED!
Biblical Answers to Some of Life's Toughest Questions
Copyright © 1993 by Rod Parsley
All rights reserved.
Printed in the United States of America.
ISBN 1-880244-12-8

Published by:
Results Publishing
World Harvest Church
P.O. Box 32932
Columbus, Ohio 43232
U.S.A.

TABLE OF CONTENTS

A PERSONAL WORD   *4*

One: **THE BASICS**

    THE BIBLE   *6*

    SALVATION   *12*

    WATER BAPTISM   *23*

    THE RAPTURE   *27*

Two: **THE HOLY GHOST**

    ...INFILLING OF   *34*

    ...GIFTS OF   *38*

    ...FRUIT OF   *56*

Three: **CHRISTIAN LIVING**

    COMMUNION   *68*

    STEWARDSHIP   *71*

    PRAYER   *83*

    WITNESSING   *88*

    FELLOWSHIP   *92*

Four: **TOUGH ISSUES**

    SOCIAL DRINKING   *96*

    HEALING, IS IT FOR TODAY?   *98*

    FORGIVENESS   *100*

    HOMOSEXUALITY   *102*

    ABORTION   *105*

    PORNOGRAPHY   *107*

    MURDER VS. KILLING IN WARTIME   *109*

CONCLUSION   *113*

A PERSONAL WORD

I receive hundreds of letters every day. Many of these letters contain questions. Desperate for truth, people write because they feel they have no other place to turn.

You may be struggling with some of these same questions. You may feel you are walking in the dark spiritually, unable to find the answers for yourself, or perhaps you just want more understanding about what the Word of God has to say.

I have coupled some of the most frequently asked questions with responses based on the ultimate authority of the Word of God.

Realize that these words come not from the theology of Rod Parsley, but directly from the inspired Word of God. I encourage you to ask the Holy Ghost to give you personal revelation as you read through this study guide.

We are to be ready to give an answer for the hope that lies within us (1 Peter 3:15), and we have been admonished to study to show ourselves approved unto God, so we will not be ashamed when others question our faith (2 Timothy 2:15).

You are not the first person to ask questions, and you won't be the last. I pray you find within these pages the answers you need. Study well, and if you lack wisdom, you have only to ask of the Father and He will give it to you (James 1:5).

Pastor Rod Parsley

One:

THE BASICS

THE BIBLE

Dear Pastor Parsley:

I became a Christian two years ago. I was told that I should read the Bible every day, but it is hard to understand. I am not doing anything wrong. I obey the Ten Commandments. I just don't like to read the Bible. Do I really need to?

I. YOU WILL RECEIVE MANY BENEFITS FROM READING THE WORD OF GOD.

    A. Life

        John 6:63 It is the spirit that quickeneth; the flesh profiteth nothing: the words that I speak unto you, they are spirit, and they are life.

    B. Health

        Proverbs 4:20 My son, attend to my words; incline thine ear unto my sayings,

        v. 22 For they are life unto those that find them, and health to all their flesh.

    C. A Guiding Light

        Psalm 119:105 Thy word is a lamp unto my feet, and a light unto my path.

    D. Food for your Spirit

        Matthew 4:4 But he answered and said, It is written, Man shall not live by bread alone, but by every word that proceedeth out of the mouth of God.

        1. The natural man needs natural food; the spirit man needs spiritual food.

            John 4:32 But he [Jesus] said unto them, I have meat to eat that ye know not of.

        2. Milk is for babies.

            1 Peter 2:2 As newborn babes desire the sincere milk of the word, that ye may grow thereby.

Hebrews 5:13 For every one that uses milk is unskilful in the word of righteousness; for he is a babe.

3.   Meat is for mature Christians.

Hebrews 5:14 But strong meat belongeth to them that are of full age, even those who by reason of use have their senses exercised to discern both good and evil.

E.   Truth

John 17:17 Sanctify them through thy truth; thy word is truth.

F.   Power

Romans 1:16 For I am not ashamed of the gospel of Christ: for it is the power of God unto salvation to every one that believeth; the Jew first, and also to the Greek.

G.   A Sword

Ephesians 6:17 And take the helmet of salvation, and the sword of the Spirit, which is the word of God.

II.   UNDERSTANDING WILL COME IF YOU READ THE BIBLE.

A.   Prayerfully

1 Corinthians 2:10 But God hath revealed them unto us by his Spirit: for the Spirit searcheth all things, yea, the deep things of God.

B.   Faithfully

Ephesians 6:18 Praying always with all prayer and supplication in the Spirit, and watching thereunto with all perseverance and supplication for all saints.

C.   Expectantly

1.   God wants you to know His will for your life.

Psalm 37:23 The steps of a good man are ordered by the Lord: and he delighteth in his way.

2.   God wants you to know about His gifts for you.

> *Matthew 7:11 If ye then, being evil, know how to give good gifts unto your children, how much more shall your Father which is in heaven give good things to them that ask him?*

3.   God wants to keep you clean.

> *Ephesians 5:26 That He might sanctify and cleanse it [the church] with the washing of water by the word.*

III.   THE BIBLE WAS WRITTEN BY INSPIRATION.

A.   Inspiration

> *2 Timothy 3:16 All scripture is given by inspiration of God, and is profitable for doctrine, for reproof, for correction, for instruction in righteousness:*
>
> *v. 17 That the man of God may be perfect, thoroughly furnished unto all good works.*

1.   The Greek translation is *God-breathed.*

2.   The special power or influence upon the hearts and minds of writers of Scripture which enabled them to make an infallible record of divine truth to men.

B.   God Used Human Instruments

> *2 Peter 1:19 We have also a more sure word of prophecy; whereunto ye do well that ye take heed, as unto a light that shineth in a dark place, until the day dawn, and the day star arise in your hearts:*
>
> *v. 20 Knowing this first, that no prophecy of the scripture is of any private interpretation.*
>
> *Hebrews 1:1 God, who at sundry times and in divers manners spake in time past unto the fathers by the prophets.*

1.   The writers did not think up things to write from their own mental reasonings, but the Holy Spirit guided them.

> *2 Peter 1:21 For the prophecy came not in old time by the will of man: but holy men of God spake as they were moved by the Holy Ghost.*

2. Neither were the writers "robots" who had no control over what they were doing as they wrote.

3. Man, in his own reasoning, would never have set such a high moral standard.

1 Peter 1:16 Because it is written, Be ye holy; for I am holy.

IV. YOU CAN VIEW THE BIBLE AS 66 SMALL BOOKS, DIVIDED INTO TWO PARTS INSTEAD OF ONE LARGE BOOK.

A. The Old Testament Contains 39 Books.

Law or Books of Moses	History	Poetry
Genesis	Joshua	Job
Exodus	Judges	Psalms
Leviticus	Ruth	Proverbs
Numbers	1 Samuel	Ecclesiastes
Deuteronomy	2 Samuel	Song of Solomon
	1 Kings	
	2 Kings	
	1 Chronicles	
	2 Chronicles	
	Ezra	
	Nehemiah	
	Esther	

Major Prophets	Minor Prophets
Isaiah	Hosea
Jeremiah	Joel
Lamentations	Amos
Ezekiel	Obadiah
Daniel	Jonah
	Micah
	Nahum
	Habakkuk
	Zephaniah
	Haggai
	Zechariah
	Malachi

B. The New Testament Contains 27 Books.

Gospels	**History**	**Paul's Letters**
Matthew	Acts	Romans
Mark		1 Corinthians
Luke		2 Corinthians
John		Galatians
		Ephesians
		Philippians
		Colossians
		1 Thessalonians
		2 Thessalonians
		1 Timothy
		2 Timothy
		Titus
		Philemon

General Epistles	**Prophecy**
Hebrews	Revelation
James	
1 Peter	
2 Peter	
1 John	
2 John	
3 John	
Jude	

C. The Bible is God's Revealed Word to Man.

Hebrews 4:12 For the word of God is quick, and powerful, and sharper than any twoedged sword, piercing even to the dividing asunder of soul and spirit, and of the joints and marrow, and is a discerner of the thoughts and intents of the heart.

Revelation 1:1 The revelation of Jesus Christ, which God gave unto him, to shew unto his servants things which must shortly come to pass; and he sent and signified it by his angel unto his servant John.

D. The Bible is a Guide to Salvation and Conduct.

1 Peter 1:23 Being born again, not of corruptible seed, but of incorruptible, by the word of God, which liveth and abideth for ever.

v. 24 For all flesh is as grass, and all the glory of man as the flower of grass. The grass withereth, and the flower thereof falleth away:

v. 25 But the word of the Lord endureth for ever. And this is the word which by the gospel is preached unto you.

E.   The Bible is the Standard for all Things.

2 Timothy 3:15 And that from a child thou hast known the holy scriptures, which are able to make thee wise unto salvation through faith which is in Christ Jesus.

1 Thessalonians 2:13 For this cause also thank we God without ceasing, because, when ye received the word of God which ye heard of us, ye received it not as the word of men, but as it is in truth, the word of God, which effectually worketh also in you that believe.

SALVATION

Dear Pastor Parsley:

Last week on your Breakthrough television program you had people come to the front of the church if they wanted salvation. Is that the same thing as being born again? Can you explain to me what really happens to someone who gets saved?

I.   THERE ARE DIFFERENT WAYS TO DESCRIBE THE SALVATION EXPERIENCE.

   A. Being Saved

   Romans 10:10 For with the heart man believeth unto righteousness; and with the mouth confession is made unto salvation.

   B. Being Born Again

   John 3:3 Jesus answered and said unto him, Verily, verily, I say unto thee, Except a man be born again, he cannot see the kingdom of God.

   C. Receiving Jesus Christ as Lord and Savior.

II. WHAT IS RECEIVED THROUGH SALVATION?

   A. Substitution: One that takes the place of another.

   1. Jesus gave His life as a ransom for many.

   Matthew 20:28 Even as the Son of man came not to be ministered unto, but to minister, and to give his life a ransom for many.

   2. The Lamb of God takes away sin.

   John 1:29 The next day John seeth Jesus coming unto him, and saith, Behold the Lamb of God, which taketh away the sin of the world.

   B. Redemption: To buy back or return to the original state of affairs.

   1. You are bought with a price.

1 Corinthians 6:19 What? know ye not that your body is the temple of the Holy Ghost which is in you, which ye have of God, and ye are not your own?

v.20 For ye are bought with a price: therefore glorify God in your body, and in your spirit, which are God's.

2.   Christ paid the price.

Galations 3:13 Christ hath redeemed us from the curse of the law, being made a curse for us.

3.   Old Testament atonement vs. New Testament redemption.

　　a.   Old Testament atonement required the blood of bulls and goats.

Hebrews 9:18 Whereupon neither the first testament was dedicated without blood.

v.19 For when Moses had spoken every precept to all the people according to the law, he took the blood of calves and of goats, with water, and scarlet wool, and hyssop, and sprinkled both the book, and all the people,

v.20 Saying, This is the blood of the testament which God hath enjoined unto you.

v.21 Moreover he sprinkled with blood both the tabernacle, and all the vessels of the ministry.

v.22 And almost all things are by the law purged with blood; and without shedding of blood is no remission.

Hebrews 10:1 For the law having a shadow of good things to come, and not the very image of the things, can never with those sacrifices which they offered year by year continually make the comers thereunto perfect.

v.2 For then would they not have ceased to be offered? because that the worshippers once purged should have had no more conscience of sins.

v.3 But in those sacrifices there is a remembrance again made of sins every year.

v.4 For it is not possible that the blood of bulls and of goats should take away sins.

b. New Testament redemption required the blood of Jesus Christ.

Hebrews 9:13 For if the blood of bulls and of goats, and the ashes of an heifer sprinkling the unclean, sanctifieth to the purifying of the flesh:

v.14 How much more shall the blood of Christ, who through the eternal Spirit offered himself without spot to God, purge your conscience from dead works to serve the living God?

v.15 And for this cause he is the mediator of the new testament, that by means of death, for the redemption of the transgressions that were under the first testament, they which are called might receive the promise of eternal inheritance.

Hebrews 9:23 It was therefore necessary that the patterns of things in the heavens should be purified with these; but the heavenly things themselves with better sacrifices than these.

v.24 For Christ is not entered into the holy places made with hands, which are the figures of the true; but into heaven itself, now to appear in the presence of God for us:

v.25 Nor yet that he should offer himself often, as the high priest entereth into the holy place every year with blood of others;

v.26 For then must he often have suffered since the foundation of the world: but now once in the end of the world hath he appeared to put away sin by the sacrifice of himself.

v.27 And as it is appointed unto men once to die, but after this the judgment:

v.28 So Christ was once offered to bear the sins of many; and unto them that look for him shall he appear the second time without sin unto salvation.

C. Propitiation: The satisfaction of God's righteous demands.

Romans 3:25 Whom God hath set forth to be a propitiation through faith in his blood, to declare his righteousness for the remission of sins that are past, through the forbearance of God.

D. Reconciliation: Exchanging hatred for friendship; the act of God which enables man to fellowship with Him.

> *2 Corinthians 5:18 And all things are of God, who hath reconciled us to himself by Jesus Christ, and hath given to us the ministry of reconciliation.*
>
> *v.19 To wit, that God was in Christ, reconciling the world unto himself, not imputing their trespasses unto them; and hath committed unto us the word of reconciliation.*

E. Forgiveness: To pardon and renounce anger or resentment against another. It also involves forgetting past sins.

> *Psalm 103:12 As far as the east is from the west, so far hath he removed our transgressions from us.*
>
> *Hebrews 10:17 And their sins and iniquities will I remember no more.*

F. Justification: The establishment of a right relationship between man and God in which God declares the sinner innocent, as if he had never sinned.

> *Romans 3:26 To declare, I say, at this time his righteousness: that he might be just, and the justifier of him which believeth in Jesus.*
>
> *1 Corinthians 6:11 And such were some of you: but ye are washed, but ye are sanctified, but ye are justified in the name of the Lord Jesus, and by the Spirit of our God.*

G. Sanctification: To be made holy and set apart for God.

> *1 Corinthians 6:11 And such were some of you: but ye are washed, but ye are sanctified, but ye are justified in the name of the Lord Jesus, and by the Spirit of our God.*
>
> *Hebrews 10:10 By the which will we are sanctified through the offering of the body of Jesus Christ once for all.*

H. Eternal Life: Union with God that is not affected by the temporal boundaries of life.

> *John 3:15 That whosoever believeth in him should not perish, but have eternal life.*

v.16 For God so loved the world, that he gave his only begotten Son, that whosoever believeth in him should not perish, but have everlasting life.

v.17 For God sent not his Son into the world to condemn the world; but that the world through him might be saved.

John 3:36 He that believeth on the Son hath everlasting life: and he that believeth not the Son shall not see life; but the wrath of God abideth on him.

III. HOW YOU RECEIVE SALVATION.

A. Repent: Turn around or turn away from. First you change your mind, then you change your behavior.

1. What do you turn away from?

   a. Sin!

   1) Rebellion toward God.

   2) Disobedience to God's Word.

   3) A wrong attitude about Jesus Christ.

John 16:9 Of sin, because they believe not on me.

   b. The nature of the devil and separation from God.

John 8:44 Ye are of your father the devil, and the lusts of your father ye will do. He was a murderer from the beginning, and abode not in the truth, because there is no truth in him. When he speaketh a lie, he speaketh of his own: for he is a liar, and the father of it.

2. What (or who) do you turn toward?

   a. Jesus Christ.

   b. The Word of God.

   c. The will of God for your life.

3. Real Repentance = Real Conversion.

    a.   No man can serve two masters.

    Matthew 6:24 No man can serve two masters: for either he will hate the one, and love the other; or else he will hold to the one, and despise the other. Ye cannot serve God and mammon.

    b.   Change occurs from the inside out.

B. Believe

    1.   How do you believe? God gives you faith to believe.

    Ephesians 2:8 For by grace are ye saved through faith; and that not of yourselves: it is the gift of God:

    v.9 Not of works, lest any man should boast.

    2.   What do you believe?

    a.   God raised Jesus from the dead and He is alive!

    Romans 10:9 That if thou shalt confess with thy mouth the Lord Jesus, and shalt believe in thine heart that God hath raised him from the dead, thou shalt be saved.

    v.10 For with the heart man believeth unto righteousness; and with the mouth confession is made unto salvation.

    b.   Jesus died for my sins, and God has forgiven them all.

    Ephesians 1:7 In whom we have redemption through his blood, the forgiveness of sins, according to the riches of his grace.

    3.   Why do you believe?

    a.   The resurrection of Jesus is the basis for biblical Christianity.

    1 Corinthians 15:12 Now if Christ be preached that he rose from the dead, how say some among you that there is no resurrection of the dead?

    v.13 But if there be no resurrection of the dead, then is Christ not risen:

    v.14 And if Christ be not risen, then is our preaching vain, and your faith is also vain.

v.15 Yea, and we are found false witnesses of God; because we have testified of God that he raised up Christ: whom he raised not up, if so be that the dead rise not.

v.16 For if the dead rise not, then is not Christ raised:

v.17 And if Christ be not raised, your faith is vain; ye are yet in your sins.

v.18 Then they also which are fallen asleep in Christ are perished.

v.19 If in this life only we have hope in Christ, we are of all men most miserable.

v.20 But now is Christ risen from the dead, and become the firstfruits of them that slept.

v.21 For since by man came death, by man came also the resurrection of the dead.

v.22 For as in Adam all die, even so in Christ shall all be made alive.

b.   It was the central theme of the preaching of the New Testament church.

    1.   In the book of Acts.

Acts 2:32 This Jesus hath God raised up, whereof we all are witnesses.

Acts 3:15 And killed the Prince of life, whom God hath raised from the dead; whereof we are witnesses.

Acts 4:10 Be it known unto you all, and to all the people of Israel, that by the name of Jesus Christ of Nazareth, whom ye crucified, whom God raised from the dead, even by him doth this man stand here before you whole.

Acts 5:30 The God of our fathers raised up Jesus, whom ye slew and hanged on a tree.

Acts 10:40 Him God raised up the third day, and shewed him openly.

Acts 13:30 But God raised him from the dead.

2. In the Epistles, the letters to the church.

   Romans 1:4 And declared to be the Son of God with power, according to the spirit of holiness, by the resurrection from the dead.

   1 Corinthians 15:1 Moreover, brethren, I declare unto you the gospel which I preached unto you, which also ye have received, and wherein ye stand;

   v.2 By which also ye are saved, if ye keep in memory what I preached unto you, unless ye have believed in vain.

   v.3 For I delivered unto you first of all that which I also received, how that Christ died for our sins according to the scriptures.

   2 Corinthians 4:14 Knowing that he which raised up the Lord Jesus shall raise up us also by Jesus, and shall present us with you.

   2 Corinthians 5:15 And that he died for all, that they which live should not henceforth live unto themselves, but unto him which died for them, and rose again.

   Ephesians 1:20 Which he wrought in Christ, when he raised him from the dead, and set him at his own right hand in the heavenly places.

   Ephesians 2:5 Even when we were dead in sins, hath quickened us together with Christ, (by grace ye are saved).

3. In the book of Revelation.

   Revelation 1:8 I am Alpha and Omega, the beginning and the ending, saith the Lord, which is, and which was, and which is to come, the Almighty.

C. Confess

1. What do you say?

   Romans 10:9 That if thou shalt confess with thy mouth the Lord Jesus, and shalt believe in thine heart that God hath raised him from the dead, thou shalt be saved.

   v.10 For with the heart man believeth unto righteousness; and with the mouth confession is made unto salvation.

a. You say what you believe.

b. You say what God's Word says.

2. Why is saying it so important?

a. There is power in testimony.

Revelation 12:11 And they overcame him by the blood of the lamb and the word of their testimony; and they loved not their lives unto death.

b. What you say is what you get.

Mark 11:22 And Jesus answering saith unto them, Have faith in God.

v.23 For verily I say unto you, That whosoever shall say unto this mountain, Be thou removed, and be thou cast into the sea; and shall not doubt in his heart, but shall believe that those things which he saith shall come to pass; he shall have whatsoever he saith.

v.24 Therefore I say unto you, What things soever ye desire, when ye pray, believe that ye receive them, and ye shall have them.

c. Your confession will cause you to operate in the principle of faith.

1) Believe it.

2) Say it.

IV. WHAT HAPPENS TO YOU INSIDE?

A. Before Salvation

1. You were spiritually dead.

Ephesians 2:2 Wherein in time past ye walked according to the course of this world, according to the prince of the power of the air, the spirit that now worketh in the children of disobedience:

v.3 Among whom also we all had our conversation in times past in the lusts of our flesh, fulfilling the desires of the flesh and of the mind; and were by nature the children of wrath, even as others.

2. You were corrupt on the inside.

Ephesians 4:22 That ye put off concerning the former conversation the old man, which is corrupt according to the deceitful lusts.

3. You were separated from God.

Ephesians 2:12 That at that time ye were without Christ, being aliens from the commonwealth of Israel, and strangers from the covenants of promise, having no hope, and without God in the world.

B. After Salvation

1. You are spiritually alive.

Colossians 2:13 And you, being dead in your sins and the uncircumcision of your flesh, hath he quickened together with him, having forgiven you all trespasses.

2. You are made holy.

1 Corinthians 1:30 But of him are ye in Christ Jesus, who of God is made unto us wisdom, and righteousness, and sanctification, and redemption.

3. You are drawn near to Christ.

Ephesians 2:13 But now in Christ Jesus ye who sometimes were far off are made nigh by the blood of Christ.

C. Scriptural Contrast

2 Corinthians 6:14 Be ye not unequally yoked together with unbelievers: for what fellowship hath righteousness with unrighteousness? and what communion hath light with darkness?

v.15 And what concord hath Christ with Belial? or what part hath he that believeth with an infidel?

v.16 And what agreement hath the temple of God with idols? for ye are the temple of the living God; as God hath said, I will dwell in them, and walk in them; and I will be their God, and they shall be my people.

Before	**Jesus Christ**	*After*
Unrighteousness		Righteous
Darkness		Light
Belial		Christ
Infidel		Believer
Idols		Temple of God

V. THE END RESULT OF SALVATION.

A. Life Everlasting

1 John 5:13 These things have I written unto you that believe on the name of the Son of God; that ye may know that ye have eternal life, and that ye may believe on the name of the Son of God.

B. Eternity in the Presence of Christ

Ecclesiastes 12:7 Then shall the dust return to the earth as it was: and the spirit shall return unto God who gave it.

Luke 23:42 And he said unto Jesus, Lord, remember me when thou comest into thy kingdom.

v.43 And Jesus said unto him, Verily I say unto thee, To day shalt thou be with me in paradise.

2 Corinthians 5:8 We are confident, I say, and willing rather to be absent from the body, and to be present with the Lord.

WATER BAPTISM

Dear Pastor Parsley:

I was raised in a denomination that believed in sprinkling for baptism. I know you teach baptism by total immersion. Since I have already been baptized by sprinkling as an infant, isn't that enough?

I. WHAT DOES IT MEAN TO BE BAPTIZED?

 A. From the Greek word *bapto* meaning to cover fully with fluid and make fully wet.

 B. You are drawing a line of separation.

 C. You are not who you used to be.

 > *2 Corinthians 5:17 Therefore if any man be in Christ, he is a new creature: old things are passed away; behold, all things are become new.*

 D. You are making a public confession.

 1. You are giving public testimony of faith in Jesus Christ.

 > *Matthew 10:32 Whosoever therefore shall confess me before men, him will I confess also before my Father which is in heaven.*

 > *v.33 But whosoever shall deny me before men, him will I also deny before my Father which is in heaven.*

 2. You are identifying with Jesus Christ.

 a. In His death.

 b. In His burial.

 c. In His resurrection.

II. WHY SHOULD I BE BAPTIZED?

 A. It is an act of obedience.

1. Jesus gave us an example to follow.

    Matthew 3:13 Then cometh Jesus from Galilee to Jordan unto John, to be baptized of him.

    v.14 But John forbad him, saying, I have need to be baptized of thee, and comest thou to me?

    v.15 And Jesus answering said unto him, Suffer it to be so now: for thus it becometh us to fulfil all righteousness. Then he suffered him.

2. Jesus gave us a commandment to follow.

    Matthew 28:19 Go ye therefore, and teach all nations, baptizing them in the name of the Father, and of the Son, and of the Holy Ghost:

    v.20 Teaching them to observe all things whatsoever I have commanded you: and, lo, I am with you alway, even unto the end of the world. Amen.

    Mark 16:16 He that believeth and is baptized shall be saved; but he that believeth not shall be damned.

B. It identifies us with the Lord Jesus Christ.

1. New Testament believers experienced much persecution as a result of their testimony for Christ.

2. We must not be afraid to give testimony of what Jesus Christ has done for us.

C. It helps seal our commitment to Christ.

1. Many Christians want to hold onto the world with one hand and onto God with the other.

2. Baptism makes it more difficult to go back to old lifestyles, patterns of behavior, etc., because it is a public declaration of your new life in God.

III. WHAT IS REQUIRED TO BE BAPTIZED?

A. You the Candidate

1. Anyone who has accepted Jesus Christ as Lord and Savior.

2. Anyone who recognizes its significance.

B.   The Element of Water.

C.   A Minister to Baptize

IV.   WHAT EXAMPLES OF BAPTISM ARE THERE IN SCRIPTURE?

A.   Jesus

> *Mark 1:9   And it came to pass in those days that Jesus came from Nazareth of Galilee, and was baptized of John in Jordan.*

B.   Ethiopian Eunuch

> *Acts 8:36   And as they went on their way, they came unto a certain water: and the eunuch said, See, here is water; what doth hinder me to be baptized?*

> *v.37   And Philip said, If thou believest with all thine heart, thou mayest.   And he answered and said, I believe that Jesus Christ is the Son of God.*

> *v.38   And he commanded the chariot to stand still: and they went down both into the water, both Philip and the eunuch; and he baptized him.*

C.   Cornelius

> *Acts 10:44   While Peter yet spake these words, the Holy Ghost fell on all them which heard the word.*

> *v.45   And they of the circumcision which believed were astonished, as many as came with Peter, because that on the Gentiles also was poured out the gift of the Holy Ghost.*

> *v.46   For they heard them speak with tongues, and magnify God. Then answered Peter,*

> *v.47   Can any man forbid water, that these should not be baptized, which have received the Holy Ghost as well as we?*

> *v.48   And he commanded them to be baptized in the name of the Lord.   Then prayed they him to tarry certain days.*

D. Philippian Jailer

> *Acts 16:30 And brought them out, and said, Sirs, what must I do to be saved?*
>
> *v.31 And they said, Believe on the Lord Jesus Christ, and thou shalt be saved, and thy house.*
>
> *v.32 And they spake unto him the word of the Lord, and to all that were in his house.*
>
> *v.33 And he took them the same hour of the night, and washed their stripes; and was baptized, he and all his, straightway.*
>
> *v.34 And when he had brought them into his house, he set meat before them, and rejoiced, believing in God with all his house.*

E. Peter

> *Acts 2:38 Then Peter said unto them, Repent, and be baptized every one of you in the name of Jesus Christ for the remission of sins, and ye shall receive the gift of the Holy Ghost.*
>
> *v.39 For the promise is unto you, and to your children, and to all that are afar off, even as many as the Lord our God shall call.*
>
> *v.40 And with many other words did he testify and exhort, saying, Save yourselves from this untoward generation.*
>
> *v.41 Then they that gladly received his word were baptized: and the same day there were added unto them about three thousand souls.*

THE RAPTURE

Dear Pastor Parsley:

I seem to be hearing a lot of talk lately about "the rapture." I am a new Christian, and I don't want to sound stupid by asking my friends at church. Is the rapture the same as the Second Coming of Christ? Can you help me understand what the rapture is?

I.   WHAT IS THE RAPTURE?

    A.   Defined from the Greek word *harpazo* meaning to seize, to catch (up away) from.

    B.   The term "rapture" is derived from the Latin verb *rapere* meaning to transport from one place to another.

    C.   It is the catching away of the saints to be with the Lord.

        1 Thessalonians 4:17 Then we which are alive and remain shall be caught up together with them in the clouds, to meet the Lord in the air: and so shall we ever be with the Lord.

II.   SCRIPTURE GIVES US SIGNS TO DISCERN WHEN IT WILL OCCUR.

        Matthew 24:3 And as he sat upon the mount of Olives, the disciples came unto him privately, saying, Tell us, when shall these things be? and what shall be the sign of thy coming, and of the end of the world?

        v.4 And Jesus answered and said unto them, Take heed that no man deceive you.

        v.5 For many shall come in my name, saying, I am Christ; and shall deceive many.

        v.6 And ye shall hear of wars and rumours of wars: see that ye be not troubled: for all these things must come to pass, but the end is not yet.

        v.7 For nation shall rise against nation, and kingdom against kingdom: and there shall be famines, and pestilences, and earthquakes, in divers places.

v.8 All these are the beginning of sorrows.

v.9 Then shall they deliver you up to be afflicted, and shall kill you: and ye shall be hated of all nations for my name's sake.

v.10 And then shall many be offended, and shall betray one another, and shall hate one another.

v.11 And many false prophets shall rise, and shall deceive many.

v.12 And because iniquity shall abound, the love of many shall wax cold.

v.13 But he that shall endure unto the end, the same shall be saved.

v.14 And this gospel of the kingdom shall be preached in all the world for a witness unto all nations; and then shall the end come.

v.15 When ye therefore shall see the abomination of desolation, spoken of by Daniel the prophet, stand in the holy place, (whoso readeth, let him understand:)

v.16 Then let them which be in Judaea flee into the mountains:

v.17 Let him which is on the housetop not come down to take any thing out of his house:

v.18 Neither let him which is in the field return back to take his clothes.

v.19 And woe unto them that are with child, and to them that give suck in those days!

v.20 But pray ye that your flight be not in the winter, neither on the sabbath day:

v.21 For then shall be great tribulation, such as was not since the beginning of the world to this time, no, nor ever shall be.

v.22 And except those days should be shortened, there should no flesh be saved: but for the elect's sake those days shall be shortened.

v.23 Then if any man shall say unto you, Lo, here is Christ, or there; believe it not.

v.24 For there shall arise false Christs, and false prophets, and shall shew great signs and wonders; insomuch that, if it were possible, they shall deceive the very elect.

v.25 Behold, I have told you before.

v.26 Wherefore if they shall say unto you, Behold, he is in the desert; go not forth: behold, he is in the secret chambers; believe it not.

v.27 For as the lightning cometh out of the east, and shineth even unto the west; so shall also the coming of the Son of man be.

v.28 For wheresoever the carcase is, there will the eagles be gathered together.

v.29 Immediately after the tribulation of those days shall the sun be darkened, and the moon shall not give her light, and the stars shall fall from heaven, and the powers of the heavens shall be shaken:

v.30 And then shall appear the sign of the Son of man in heaven: and then shall all the tribes of the earth mourn, and they shall see the Son of man coming in the clouds of heaven with power and great glory.

v.31 And he shall send his angels with a great sound of a trumpet, and they shall gather together his elect from the four winds, from one end of heaven to the other.

v.32 Now learn a parable of the fig tree; When his branch is yet tender, and putteth forth leaves, ye know that summer is nigh:

v.33 So likewise ye, when ye shall see all these things, know that it is near, even at the doors.

v.34 Verily I say unto you, This generation shall not pass, till all these things be fulfilled.

v.35 Heaven and earth shall pass away, but my words shall not pass away.

v.36 But of that day and hour knoweth no man, no, not the angels of heaven, but my Father only.

v.37 But as the days of Noe were, so shall also the coming of the Son of man be.

v.38 For as in the days that were before the flood they were eating and drinking, marrying and giving in marriage, until the day that Noe entered into the ark,

v.39 And knew not until the flood came, and took them all away; so shall also the coming of the Son of man be.

v.40 Then shall two be in the field; the one shall be taken, and the other left.

v.41 Two women shall be grinding at the mill; the one shall be taken, and the other left.

v.42 Watch therefore: for ye know not what hour your Lord doth come.

v.43 But know this, that if the goodman of the house had known in what watch the thief would come, he would have watched, and would not have suffered his house to be broken up.

v.44 Therefore be ye also ready: for in such an hour as ye think not the Son of man cometh.

Luke 17:26 And as it was in the days of Noe, so shall it be also in the days of the Son of man.

v.27 They did eat, they drank, they married wives, they were given in marriage, until the day that Noe entered into the ark, and the flood came, and destroyed them all.

v.28 Likewise also as it was in the days of Lot; they did eat, they drank, they bought, they sold, they planted, they builded;

v.29 But the same day that Lot went out of Sodom it rained fire and brimstone from heaven, and destroyed them all.

v.30 Even thus shall it be in the day when the Son of man is revealed.

v.31 In that day, he which shall be upon the housetop, and his stuff in the house, let him not come down to take it away: and he that is in the field, let him likewise not return back.

v.32 Remember Lot's wife.

v.33 Whosoever shall seek to save his life shall lose it; and whosoever shall lose his life shall preserve it.

v.34 I tell you, in that night there shall be two men in one bed; the one shall be taken, and the other shall be left.

v.35 Two women shall be grinding together; the one shall be taken, and the other left.

v.36 Two men shall be in the field; the one shall be taken, and the other left.

v.37 And they answered and said unto him, Where, Lord? And he said unto them, Wheresoever the body is, thither will the eagles be gathered together.

III. SCRIPTURE TELLS US THE PURPOSE OF THE RAPTURE.

A. To Spare the Saints

1 Thessalonians 1:9 For they themselves shew of us what manner of entering in we had unto you, and how ye turned to God from idols to serve the living and true God;

v.10 And to wait for his Son from heaven, whom he raised from the dead, even Jesus, which delivered us from the wrath to come.

Revelation 3:10 Because thou hast kept the word of my patience, I also will keep thee from the hour of temptation, which shall come upon all the world, to try them that dwell upon the earth.

B. To Change the Saints

1 Corinthians 15:51 Behold, I shew you a mystery; We shall not all sleep, but we shall all be changed,

v.52 In a moment, in the twinkling of an eye, at the last trump: for the trumpet shall sound, and the dead shall be raised incorruptible, and we shall be changed.

v.53 For this corruptible must put on incorruption, and this mortal must put on immortality.

C.   To Give Hope and Comfort to the Saints

1 Thessalonians 4:16 For the Lord himself shall descend from heaven with a shout, with the voice of the archangel, and with the trump of God: and the dead in Christ shall rise first:

v.17 Then we which are alive and remain shall be caught up together with them in the clouds, to meet the Lord in the air: and so shall we ever be with the Lord.

v.18 Wherefore comfort one another with these words.

Two:

THE HOLY GHOST

THE HOLY GHOST
...INFILLING OF

Dear Pastor Parsley:

I want to know more about this Holy Ghost you talk about. Can it help me live right? I am saved, but I'm afraid to tell anyone because I mess up so much. Can I receive the Holy Ghost? I need help soon!

I. WHAT IS THE BAPTISM IN THE HOLY GHOST?

  A. It is an enduement of power from God.

  Luke 24:49 And, behold, I send the promise of my Father upon you: but tarry ye in the city of Jerusalem, until ye be endued with power from on high.

  B. It is an experience subsequent to salvation.

  Acts 2:1 And when the day of Pentecost was fully come, they were all with one accord in one place.

  v.2 And suddenly there came a sound from heaven as of a rushing mighty wind, and it filled all the house where they were sitting.

  v.3 And there appeared unto them cloven tongues like as of fire, and it sat upon each of them.

  v.4 And they were all filled with the Holy Ghost, and began to speak with other tongues, as the Spirit gave them utterance.

  Acts 8:12 But when they believed Philip preaching the things concerning the kingdom of God, and the name of Jesus Christ, they were baptized, both men and women.

  Acts 8:15 Who, when they were come down, prayed for them, that they might receive the Holy Ghost.

  Acts 8:17 Then laid they their hands on them, and they received the Holy Ghost.

C. It is part of Jesus' ministry to you.

> *Luke 3:16 John answered, saying unto them all, I indeed baptize you with water; but one mightier than I cometh, the latchet of whose shoes I am not worthy to unloose: he shall baptize you with the Holy Ghost and with fire.*

D. It was prophesied by the prophet Joel.

> *Acts 2:16 But this is that which was spoken by the prophet Joel.*

II. WHO QUALIFIES?

A. You qualify.

1. The Holy Ghost came to dwell within you when you were born again.

> *Romans 8:16 The Spirit itself beareth witness with our spirit, that we are the children of God.*

2. The Holy Ghost will not only be with you, but in you.

> *John 14:16 And I will pray the Father, and he shall give you another Comforter, that he may abide with you for ever;*
>
> *v.17 Even the Spirit of truth; whom the world cannot receive, because it seeth him not, neither knoweth him: but ye know him; for he dwelleth with you, and shall be in you.*

B. Those who follow after you in faith qualify.

> *Acts 2:39 For the promise is unto you, and to your children, and to all that are afar off, even as many as the Lord our God shall call.*

III. HOW WILL IT HELP ME?

A. The Holy Ghost supplies power.

1. He supplies miracle-working power.

> *Acts 1:8 But ye shall receive power, after that the Holy Ghost is come upon you: and ye shall be witnesses unto me both in Jerusalem, and in all Judaea, and in Samaria, and unto the uttermost part of the earth.*

2. He supplies power to live right.

> *John 16:13 Howbeit when he, the Spirit of truth, is come, he will guide you into all truth: for he shall not speak of himself; but whatsoever he shall hear, that shall he speak: and he will shew you things to come.*

B. The Holy Ghost brings comfort.

> *John 14:16 And I will pray the Father, and he shall give you another Comforter, that he may abide with you for ever.*

> *John 14:26 But the Comforter, which is the Holy Ghost, whom the Father will send in my name, he shall teach you all things, and bring all things to your remembrance, whatsoever I have said unto you.*

> *John 15:26 But when the Comforter is come, whom I will send unto you from the Father, even the Spirit of truth, which proceedeth from the Father, he shall testify of me.*

> *John 16:7 Nevertheless I tell you the truth; It is expedient for you that I go away: for if I go not away, the Comforter will not come unto you; but if I depart, I will send him unto you.*

C. The Holy Ghost gives us power to be witnesses.

1. A witness to an event is someone who produces proof that what he is saying is true.

2. We are saying Jesus is alive.

> *Acts 4:33 And with great power gave the apostles witness of the resurrection of the Lord Jesus: and great grace was upon them all.*

D. The Holy Ghost gives new understanding of the Word of God.

> *John 16:13 Howbeit when he, the Spirit of truth, is come, he will guide you into all truth: for he shall not speak of himself; but whatsoever he shall hear, that shall he speak: and he will shew you things to come.*

E. The Holy Ghost gives us the ability to speak in other tongues.

1. Speaking in tongues will build you spiritually.

Jude 20 But ye, beloved, building up yourselves on your most holy faith, praying in the Holy Ghost.

2. Speaking in tongues will enable more effective prayer.

Romans 8:26 Likewise the Spirit also helpeth our infirmities: for we know not what we should pray for as we ought: but the Spirit itself maketh intercession for us with groanings which cannot be uttered.

v.27 And he that searcheth the hearts knoweth what is the mind of the Spirit, because he maketh intercession for the saints according to the will of God.

3. Speaking in tongues is an additional means of communication with God.

1 Corinthians 14:2 For he that speaketh in an unknown tongue speaketh not unto men, but unto God: for no man understandeth him; howbeit in the spirit he speaketh mysteries.

4. Speaking in tongues gives access to all the gifts of the Spirit.

1 Corinthians 12:8 For to one is given by the Spirit the word of wisdom; to another the word of knowledge by the same Spirit;

v.9 To another faith by the same Spirit; to another the gifts of healing by the same Spirit;

v.10 To another the working of miracles; to another prophecy; to another discerning of spirits; to another divers kinds of tongues; to another the interpretation of tongues.

THE HOLY GHOST
...GIFTS OF

Dear Pastor Parsley:

I believe I was filled with the Holy Ghost when you prayed for people on your television broadcast, but I don't know if I have any of the gifts that are supposed to come with that experience. I need to know more about the gifts of the Spirit. I want to do something with what I now feel inside.

I.   REVELATION GIFTS - GIFTS THAT KNOW SOMETHING.

    A.   Word of Wisdom

       1.   What is wisdom?

          Understanding what is true, right or lasting — not to be confused with knowledge, which is an accumulation of information.

       2.   What is the word of wisdom?

          Supernatural insight into or revelation about the plans and purposes of God.

       3.   What are the distinctive characteristics of the word of wisdom?

          a.   It is a specific word of God's wisdom, not just wisdom in general.

          b.   It deals with things in the future, not the present or the past.

          c.   It is different than ordinary guidance from God.

       4.   We can learn about the word of wisdom by studying examples in the Bible.

          a.   Old Testament

            1)   Noah

Genesis 6:17 And, behold, I, even I, do bring a flood of waters upon the earth, to destroy all flesh, wherein is the breath of life, from under heaven; and every thing that is in the earth shall die.

v.18 But with thee will I establish my covenant; and thou shalt come into the ark, thou, and thy sons, and thy wife, and thy sons' wives with thee.

v.19 And of every living thing of all flesh, two of every sort shalt thou bring into the ark, to keep them alive with thee; they shall be male and female.

v.20 Of fowls after their kind, and of cattle after their kind, of every creeping thing of the earth after his kind, two of every sort shall come unto thee, to keep them alive.

v.21 And take thou unto thee of all food that is eaten, and thou shalt gather it to thee; and it shall be for food for thee, and for them.

v.22 Thus did Noah; according to all that God commanded him, so did he.

2) Joseph

Genesis 37:5 And Joseph dreamed a dream, and he told it his brethren: and they hated him yet the more.

v.6 And he said unto them, Hear, I pray you, this dream which I have dreamed:

v.7 For, behold, we were binding sheaves in the field, and, lo, my sheaf arose, and also stood upright; and, behold, your sheaves stood round about, and made obeisance to my sheaf.

v.8 And his brethren said to him, Shalt thou indeed reign over us? or shalt thou indeed have dominion over us? And they hated him yet the more for his dreams, and for his words.

v.9 And he dreamed yet another dream, and told it his brethren, and said, Behold, I have dreamed a dream more; and, behold, the sun and the moon and the eleven stars made obeisance to me.

v.10 And he told it to his father, and to his brethren: and his father rebuked him, and said unto him, What is this dream that thou hast dreamed? Shall I and thy mother and thy brethren indeed come to bow down ourselves to thee to the earth?

v.11 And his brethren envied him; but his father observed the saying.

b. New Testament

1) Examples in the ministry of Jesus

a)   Jesus knew about Peter's denial before it happened.

Luke 22:31   And the Lord said, Simon, Simon, behold, Satan hath desired to have you, that he may sift you as wheat:

v.32   But I have prayed for thee, that thy faith fail not: and when thou art converted, strengthen thy brethren.

v.33   And he said unto him, Lord, I am ready to go with thee, both into prison, and to death.

v.34   And he said, I tell thee, Peter, the cock shall not crow this day, before that thou shalt thrice deny that thou knowest me.

b)   Jesus knew about His upcoming death, burial and resurrection.

Matthew 20:17   And Jesus going up to Jerusalem took the twelve disciples apart in the way, and said unto them,

v.18   Behold, we go up to Jerusalem; and the Son of man shall be betrayed unto the chief priests and unto the scribes, and they shall condemn him to death,

v.19   And shall deliver him to the Gentiles to mock, and to scourge, and to crucify him: and the third day he shall rise again.

2)   Examples in other ministries

a)   Ananias and Paul

Acts 9:15   But the Lord said unto him, Go thy way: for he is a chosen vessel unto me, to bear my name before the Gentiles, and kings, and the children of Israel.

b)   Agabus and Paul

Acts 21:10   And as we tarried there many days, there came down from Judaea a certain prophet, named Agabus.

v.11   And when he was come unto us, he took Paul's girdle, and bound his own hands and feet, and said, Thus saith the Holy Ghost, So shall the Jews at Jerusalem bind the man that owneth this girdle, and shall deliver him into the hands of the Gentiles.

B. Word of Knowledge

1. What is knowledge?

   An accumulation of facts about a given subject.

2. What is the word of knowledge?

   Supernatural revelation of facts concerning people, places or things — present or past.

3. What are the distinctive characteristics of the Word of Knowledge?

   a. It deals with the present or the past, never the future (do not confuse with the word of wisdom).

   b. It is a specific word of knowledge, not just knowledge in general.

   c. It is knowledge given by God, which the recipient has no other way of knowing.

   d. As with word of wisdom, this is separate from "ordinary" guidance.

4. We can learn about the word of knowledge from Biblical examples.

   a. Old Testament

      1) Kish's donkeys

   1 Samuel 9:20 And as for thine asses that were lost three days ago, set not thy mind on them; for they are found. And on whom is all the desire of Israel? Is it not on thee, and on all thy father's house?

      2) Elisha and Gehazi

   2 Kings 5:25 But he went in, and stood before his master. And Elisha said unto him, Whence comest thou, Gehazi? And he said, Thy servant went no whither.

   v.26 And he said unto him, Went not mine heart with thee, when the man turned again from his chariot to meet thee? Is it a time to receive money, and to receive garments, and oliveyards, and vineyards, and sheep, and oxen, and menservants, and maidservants?

   b. New Testament

      1) Jesus knew about the woman at the well.

John 4:16 Jesus saith unto her, Go, call thy husband, and come hither.

v.17 The woman answered and said, I have no husband. Jesus said unto her, Thou hast well said, I have no husband:

v.18 For thou hast had five husbands; and he whom thou now hast is not thy husband: in that saidst thou truly.

    2) Peter knew people from Cornelius' house had arrived to see him.

Acts 10:19 While Peter thought on the vision, the Spirit said unto him, Behold, three men seek thee.

C. Discerning of Spirits

  1. What does "discerning" mean?

    To recognize or perceive, to see clearly.

  2. What is the discerning of spirits?

    Supernatural insight into the realm of the spirit.

  3. What are the distinctive characteristics of the discerning of spirits?

    a. God and the holy angels can be perceived.

    b. The devil and evil spirits can be perceived.

    c. The intents of the hearts of people can be perceived.

II. POWER GIFTS — GIFTS THAT DO SOMETHING.

  A. The Gift Of Faith

    1. What is faith?

      Faith is knowing God and trusting in God.

    2. What is the gift of faith?

      Special wonder-working faith; supernatural, unwavering trust in God which enables the possessor to receive a miracle.

3.   What are the distinctive characteristics of the gift of faith?

   a.   A miracle is received.

   b.   A human instrument is not used; it is all God.

   c.   In many cases an element of danger is involved.

4.   We can learn about the gift of faith by studying examples in the Bible.

   a.   Jesus

   Luke 8:22 Now it came to pass on a certain day, that he went into a ship with his disciples: and he said unto them, Let us go over unto the other side of the lake. And they launched forth.

      1)   Sleeping during the storm while the boat was filling with water was the gift of faith.

   v.23 But as they sailed he fell asleep: and there came down a storm of wind on the lake; and they were filled with water, and were in jeopardy.

      2)   Rebuking the wind and the sea was a miracle.

   v.24 And they came to him, and awoke him, saying, Master, master, we perish. Then he arose, and rebuked the wind and the raging of the water: and they ceased, and there was a calm.

   b.   Elijah fed by ravens

   1 Kings 17:2 And the word of the Lord came unto him, saying,

   v.3 Get thee hence, and turn thee eastward, and hide thyself by the brook Cherith, that is before Jordan.

   v.4 And it shall be, that thou shalt drink of the brook; and I have commanded the ravens to feed thee there.

   v.5 So he went and did according unto the word of the Lord: for he went and dwelt by the brook Cherith, that is before Jordan.

   v.6 And the ravens brought him bread and flesh in the morning, and bread and flesh in the evening; and he drank of the brook.

c. Hebrew men in the fiery furnace

Daniel 3:13 Then Nebuchadnezzar in his rage and fury commanded to bring Shadrach, Meshach, and Abednego. Then they brought these men before the king.

v.14 Nebuchadnezzar spake and said unto them, Is it true, O Shadrach, Meshach, and Abednego, do not ye serve my gods, nor worship the golden image which I have set up?

v.15 Now if ye be ready that at what time ye hear the sound of the cornet, flute, harp, sackbut, psaltery, and dulcimer, and all kinds of musick, ye fall down and worship the image which I have made; well: but if ye worship not, ye shall be cast the same hour into the midst of a burning fiery furnace; and who is that God that shall deliver you out of my hands?

v.16 Shadrach, Meshach, and Abednego, answered and said to the king, O Nebuchadnezzar, we are not careful to answer thee in this matter.

v.17 If it be so, our God whom we serve is able to deliver us from the burning fiery furnace, and he will deliver us out of thine hand, O king.

v.18 But if not, be it known unto thee, O king, that we will not serve thy gods, nor worship the golden image which thou hast set up.

v.19 Then was Nebuchadnezzar full of fury, and the form of his visage was changed against Shadrach, Meshach, and Abednego: therefore he spake, and commanded that they should heat the furnace one seven times more than it was wont to be heated.

v.20 And he commanded the most mighty men that were in his army to bind Shadrach, Meshach, and Abednego, and to cast them into the burning fiery furnace.

v.21 Then these men were bound in their coats, their hosen, and their hats, and their other garments, and were cast into the midst of the burning fiery furnace.

v.22 Therefore because the king's commandment was urgent, and the furnace exceeding hot, the flame of the fire slew those men that took up Shadrach, Meshach, and Abednego.

v.23 And these three men, Shadrach, Meshach, and Abednego, fell down bound into the midst of the burning fiery furnace.

v.24 Then Nebuchadnezzar the king was astonied, and rose up in haste, and spake, and said unto his counsellors, Did not we cast three men bound into the midst of the fire? They answered and said unto the king, True, O king.

v.25 He answered and said, Lo, I see four men loose, walking in the midst of the fire, and they have no hurt; and the form of the fourth is like the Son of God.

v.26 Then Nebuchadnezzar came near to the mouth of the burning fiery furnace, and spake, and said, Shadrach, Meshach, and Abednego, ye servants of the most high God, come forth, and come hither. Then Shadrach, Meshach, and Abednego, came forth of the midst of the fire.

d.   Daniel in the lion's den

Daniel 6:16 Then the king commanded, and they brought Daniel, and cast him into the den of lions. Now the king spake and said unto Daniel, Thy God whom thou servest continually, he will deliver thee.

v.17 And a stone was brought, and laid upon the mouth of the den; and the king sealed it with his own signet, and with the signet of his lords; that the purpose might not be changed concerning Daniel.

v.18 Then the king went to his palace, and passed the night fasting: neither were instruments of musick brought before him: and his sleep went from him.

v.19 Then the king arose very early in the morning, and went in haste unto the den of lions.

v.20 And when he came to the den, he cried with a lamentable voice unto Daniel: and the king spake and said to Daniel, O Daniel, servant of the living God, is thy God, whom thou servest continually, able to deliver thee from the lions?

v.21 Then said Daniel unto the king, O king, live for ever.

v.22 My God hath sent his angel, and hath shut the lions' mouths, that they have not hurt me: forasmuch as before him innocency was found in me; and also before thee, O king, have I done no hurt.

v.23 Then was the king exceeding glad for him, and commanded

that they should take Daniel up out of the den. So Daniel was taken up out of the den, and no manner of hurt was found upon him, because he believed in his God.

v.24 And the king commanded, and they brought those men which had accused Daniel, and they cast them into the den of lions, them, their children, and their wives; and the lions had the mastery of them, and brake all their bones in pieces or ever they came at the bottom of the den.

B. Working of Miracles

   1. What is a miracle?

      Something that happens contrary to the known laws of science or nature.

   2. What is the working of miracles?

      The supernatural intervention of God, using an instrument (usually a human being) in which the laws of nature are suspended, altered or controlled.

   3. What are the distinctive characteristics of the working of miracles?

      a. God uses the one through whom the gift operates to actually "work" the miracle.

      b. An instrument, human or otherwise, is always involved.

   4. We can learn about the working of miracles by studying examples from the Bible.

      a. Old Testament

         1) Moses parting the Red Sea

         Exodus 14:21 And Moses stretched out his hand over the sea; and the Lord caused the sea to go back by a strong east wind all that night, and made the sea dry land, and the waters were divided.

         v.22 And the children of Israel went into the midst of the sea upon the dry ground: and the waters were a wall unto them on their right hand, and on their left.

         2) Joshua commanding the sun and moon to stand still

Joshua 10:12 Then spake Joshua to the Lord in the day when the Lord delivered up the Amorites before the children of Israel, and he said in the sight of Israel, Sun, stand thou still upon Gibeon; and thou, Moon, in the valley of Ajalon.

v.13 And the sun stood still, and the moon stayed, until the people had avenged themselves upon their enemies. Is not this written in the book of Jasher? So the sun stood still in the midst of heaven, and hasted not to go down about a whole day.

3)   Samuel calling forth thunder and lightning

1 Samuel 12:16 Now therefore stand and see this great thing, which the Lord will do before your eyes.

v.17 Is it not wheat harvest to day? I will call unto the Lord, and he shall send thunder and rain; that ye may perceive and see that your wickedness is great, which ye have done in the sight of the Lord, in asking you a king.

v.18 So Samuel called unto the Lord; and the Lord sent thunder and rain that day: and all the people greatly feared the Lord and Samuel.

v.19 And all the people said unto Samuel, Pray for thy servants unto the Lord thy God, that we die not: for we have added unto all our sins this evil, to ask us a king.

b.   New Testament

1)   Jesus turns water into wine

John 2:1 And the third day there was a marriage in Cana of Galilee; and the mother of Jesus was there:

v.2 And both Jesus was called, and his disciples, to the marriage.

v.3 And when they wanted wine, the mother of Jesus saith unto him, They have no wine.

v.4 Jesus saith unto her, Woman, what have I to do with thee? mine hour is not yet come.

v.5 His mother saith unto the servants, Whatsoever he saith unto you, do it.

v.6 And there were set there six waterpots of stone, after the manner of the purifying of the Jews, containing two or three firkins apiece.

v.7 Jesus saith unto them, Fill the waterpots with water. And they filled them up to the brim.

v.8 And he saith unto them, Draw out now, and bear unto the governor of the feast. And they bare it.

v.9 When the ruler of the feast had tasted the water that was made wine, and knew not whence it was: (but the servants which drew the water knew;) the governor of the feast called the bridegroom,

v.10 And saith unto him, Every man at the beginning doth set forth good wine; and when men have well drunk, then that which is worse: but thou hast kept the good wine until now.

v.11 This beginning of miracles did Jesus in Cana of Galilee, and manifested forth his glory; and his disciples believed on him.

2) Peter and Ananias and Sapphira

Acts 5:1 But a certain man named Ananias, with Sapphira his wife, sold a possession,

v.2 And kept back part of the price, his wife also being privy to it, and brought a certain part, and laid it at the apostles' feet.

v.3 But Peter said, Ananias, why hath Satan filled thine heart to lie to the Holy Ghost, and to keep back part of the price of the land?

v.4 Whiles it remained, was it not thine own? and after it was sold, was it not in thine own power? why hast thou conceived this thing in thine heart? thou hast not lied unto men, but unto God.

v.5 And Ananias hearing these words fell down, and gave up the ghost: and great fear came on all them that heard these things.

v.6 And the young men arose, wound him up, and carried him out, and buried him.

v.7 And it was about the space of three hours after, when his wife, not knowing what was done, came in.

v.8 And Peter answered unto her, Tell me whether ye sold the land

for so much? And she said, Yea, for so much.

v.9 Then Peter said unto her, How is it that ye have agreed together to tempt the Spirit of the Lord? behold, the feet of them which have buried thy husband are at the door, and shall carry thee out.

v.10 Then fell she down straightway at his feet, and yielded up the ghost: and the young men came in, and found her dead, and, carrying her forth, buried her by her husband.

v.11 And great fear came upon all the church, and upon as many as heard these things.

    3) Any believer

John 14:12 Verily, verily, I say unto you, He that believeth on me, the works that I do shall he do also; and greater works than these shall he do; because I go unto my Father.

C. Gifts Of Healing

  1. What is healing?

The recovery from sickness or disease. God has provided many ways for people to be healed.

    a. Believing God's Word for yourself

Mark 11:23 For verily I say unto you, That whosoever shall say unto this mountain, Be thou removed, and be thou cast into the sea; and shall not doubt in his heart, but shall believe that those things which he saith shall come to pass; he shall have whatsoever he saith.

    b. Prayer of faith

James 5:15 And the prayer of faith shall save the sick, and the Lord shall raise him up; and if he have committed sins, they shall be forgiven him.

v.16 Confess your faults one to another, and pray one for another, that ye may be healed. The effectual fervent prayer of a righteous man availeth much.

    c. Laying on of hands

Mark 16:18 They shall take up serpents; and if they drink any deadly

thing, it shall not hurt them; they shall lay hands on the sick, and they shall recover.

Acts 28:8 And it came to pass, that the father of Publius lay sick of a fever and of a bloody flux: to whom Paul entered in, and prayed, and laid his hands on him, and healed him.

    d.   Anointing with oil

James 5:14 Is any sick among you? let him call for the elders of the church; and let them pray over him, anointing him with oil in the name of the Lord.

2.   What are the gifts of healing?

Supernatural healing of sicknesses or diseases.

3.   What are the distinctive characteristics of the gifts of healing?

    a.   They differ from "ordinary" healing.

    b.   They are manifested as the Spirit wills.

4.   We can learn about the gifts of healing by studying examples from the Bible.

    a.   Old Testament

        1)   Brass serpent

Numbers 21:6 And the Lord sent fiery serpents among the people, and they bit the people; and much people of Israel died.

v.7 Therefore the people came to Moses, and said, We have sinned, for we have spoken against the Lord, and against thee; pray unto the Lord, that he take away the serpents from us. And Moses prayed for the people.

v.8 And the Lord said unto Moses, Make thee a fiery serpent, and set it upon a pole: and it shall come to pass, that every one that is bitten, when he looketh upon it, shall live.

v.9 And Moses made a serpent of brass, and put it upon a pole, and it came to pass, that if a serpent had bitten any man, when he beheld the serpent of brass, he lived.

2) Naaman the leper

2 Kings 5:8 And it was so, when Elisha the man of God had heard that the king of Israel had rent his clothes, that he sent to the king, saying, Wherefore hast thou rent thy clothes? let him come now to me, and he shall know that there is a prophet in Israel.

v.9 So Naaman came with his horses and with his chariot, and stood at the door of the house of Elisha.

v.10 And Elisha sent a messenger unto him, saying, Go and wash in Jordan seven times, and thy flesh shall come again to thee, and thou shalt be clean.

v.11 But Naaman was wroth, and went away, and said, Behold, I thought, He will surely come out to me, and stand, and call on the name of the Lord his God, and strike his hand over the place, and recover the leper.

v.12 Are not Abana and Pharpar, rivers of Damascus, better than all the waters of Israel? may I not wash in them, and be clean? So he turned and went away in a rage.

v.13 And his servants came near, and spake unto him, and said, My father, if the prophet had bid thee do some great thing, wouldest thou not have done it? how much rather then, when he saith to thee, Wash, and be clean?

v.14 Then went he down, and dipped himself seven times in Jordan, according to the saying of the man of God: and his flesh came again like unto the flesh of a little child, and he was clean.

b. New Testament

1) Jesus' ministry

a) Multitudes

Matthew 4:23 And Jesus went about all Galilee, teaching in their synagogues, and preaching the gospel of the kingdom, and healing all manner of sickness and all manner of disease among the people.

v.24 And his fame went throughout all Syria: and they brought unto him all sick people that were taken with divers diseases and torments, and those which were possessed with devils, and those which were lunatick, and those that had the palsy; and he healed them.

  b) A leper

Matthew 8:2 And, behold, there came a leper and worshipped him, saying, Lord, if thou wilt, thou canst make me clean.

v.3 And Jesus put forth his hand, and touched him, saying, I will; be thou clean. And immediately his leprosy was cleansed.

  c) People in Samaria

Acts 8:7 For unclean spirits, crying with loud voice, came out of many that were possessed with them: and many taken with palsies, and that were lame, were healed.

III. INSPIRATION GIFTS — GIFTS THAT SAY SOMETHING.

A. Gift of Prophecy

1. What is the gift of prophecy?

A divinely-inspired utterance in a known language.

2. What are the distinctive characteristics of the gift of prophecy?

  a. It is not the same as prophecy given through one who walks in the office of a prophet.

    1) A prophet is one who operates in one of the fivefold ministry gifts.

Ephesians 4:11 And he gave some, apostles; and some, prophets; and some, evangelists; and some, pastors and teachers;

    2) A prophet has a specific call from the Lord; any believer can operate in the simple gift of prophecy.

  b. In the Old Testament, prophecy involved the foretelling of events.

  c. There is no foretelling in the New Testament gift of prophecy.

  d. In the New Testament, the simple gift of prophecy is "forthtelling" — speaking inspired words of edification, exhortation, and comfort.

1 Corinthians 14:3 But he that prophesieth speaketh unto men to

edification, and exhortation, and comfort.

e. The gift of prophecy is not intended as a means of guidance and direction for New Testament believers. In every case, it will be used only to confirm what is already in a person's heart.

f. Principles governing the use of the gift of prophecy

1 Corinthians 14:1 Follow after charity, and desire spiritual gifts, but rather that ye may prophesy.

v.2 For he that speaketh in an unknown tongue speaketh not unto men, but unto God: for no man understandeth him; howbeit in the spirit he speaketh mysteries.

v.3 But he that prophesieth speaketh unto men to edification, and exhortation, and comfort.

v.4 He that speaketh in an unknown tongue edifieth himself; but he that prophesieth edifieth the church.

v.22 Wherefore tongues are for a sign, not to them that believe, but to them that believe not: but prophesying serveth not for them that believe not, but for them which believe.

3. We can learn about the gift of prophecy by studying examples from the Bible.

a. Old Testament prophecy

Genesis 3:15 And I will put enmity between thee and the woman, and between thy seed and her seed; it shall bruise thy head, and thou shalt bruise his heel.

b. New Testament gift of prophecy

1) Believers in Ephesus

Acts 19:6 And when Paul had laid his hands upon them, the Holy Ghost came on them; and they spake with tongues, and prophesied.

2) Philip's daughter

Acts 21:9 And the same man had four daughters, virgins, which did prophesy.

B. Diverse Kinds of Tongues

1. What is tongues?

   Speaking in a language inspired by the Holy Ghost, but unknown to the speaker. Tongues is the initial evidence of the baptism in the Holy Ghost.

2. What is the gift of tongues?

   A public utterance in other tongues, accompanied by an interpretation of that tongue so that the hearers may benefit.

3. What are the distinctive characteristics of the gift of tongues?

   a. Tongues and interpretation of tongues always appear together when used in public assembly. This use is distinct from the corporate use of tongues in praise and worship, which requires no interpretation.

   b. On occasion, the tongue, though unknown to the speaker, is the known language of the hearer.

   Acts 2:6 Now when this was noised abroad, the multitude came together, and were confounded, because that every man heard them speak in his own language.

   v.7 And they were all amazed and marvelled, saying one to another, Behold, are not all these which speak Galilaeans?

   v.8 And how hear we every man in our own tongue, wherein we were born?

C. Gift of Interpretation of Tongues

1. What is interpretation?

   An explanation of the meaning of something said or done.

2. What is the gift of interpretation of tongues?

   A supernatural showing forth of the meaning of an utterance in tongues, not translation word-for-word but a revealing of the meaning.

3. What are the distinctives of the gift of interpretation of tongues?

   a. Tongues and interpretation of tongues equal the gift of prophecy.

b. They were not seen in operation until the day of Pentecost.

c. Principles governing the use of tongues and interpretation of tongues are found in 1 Corinthians 14:13-15, 27-28.

4. We can learn more about tongues and interpretation of tongues by studying examples from the Bible.

a. Old Testament

1) Not in evidence

2) The prophets foretold these gifts would come to pass.

Isaiah 28:11 For with stammering lips and another tongue will he speak to this people.

Joel 2:28 And it shall come to pass afterward, that I will pour out my spirit upon all flesh; and your sons and your daughters shall prophesy, your old men shall dream dreams, your young men shall see visions:

v.29 And also upon the servants and upon the handmaids in those days will I pour out my spirit.

b. New Testament

Acts 19:6 And when Paul had laid his hands upon them, the Holy Ghost came on them; and they spake with tongues, and prophesied.

THE HOLY GHOST
...FRUITS OF

Dear Pastor Parsley:

I was raised in a Pentecostal home and filled with the Holy Ghost when I was very young. I have seen or heard every gift of the Spirit in operation in my lifetime, and I have been used in some of the gifts. My heart is grieved that I see so little of this fruit of the Spirit in the lives of Spirit-filled believers. Will you please teach more on the fruit? I think we need to be reminded of its importance.

> *Gal 5:22 But the fruit of the Spirit is love, joy, peace, longsuffering, gentleness, goodness, faith,*
>
> *v.23 Meekness, temperance: against such there is no law.*

I. LOVE

   A. Intense affection.

   B. The Greek language distinguishes three types of love based on the different aspects of man.

      1. *Eros*

         a. Love based on the passions of the flesh.

         b. Physical attraction.

      2. *Phileo*

         a. Brotherly love and civic duty based on responsible thinking.

> *1 Peter 1:22 Seeing ye have purified your souls in obeying the truth through the Spirit unto unfeigned love of the brethren, see that ye love one another with a pure heart fervently.*
>
> *Romans 12:10 Be kindly affectioned one to another with brotherly love; in honour preferring one another.*

         b. Paternal love as between a loving father and his children.

> *Revelation 3:19 As many as I love, I rebuke and chasten: be zealous therefore, and repent.*

3. *Agape*

    a. Unconquerable benevolence.

    b. The God kind of love that would lay down its life for the one it loves.

1 John 4:8 He that loveth not knoweth not God; for God is love.

John 3:16 For God so loved the world, that he gave his only begotten Son, that whosoever believeth in him should not perish, but have everlasting life.

II. JOY

A. From the Greek word *chara,* which means delight, gladness and benefit.

B. Joy is not the same as happiness.

    1. Happiness comes from "happenings."

    2. Joy comes from within your heart.

C. Joy is not an emotion.

    1. Joy is a commandment; emotions cannot be commanded.

    Philippians 4:4 Rejoice in the Lord alway: and again I say rejoice.

    2. Joy is a decision to act on God's Word.

D. You can experience joy.

    1. In His presence.

    Psalm 16:11 Thou wilt shew me the path of life: in thy presence is fulness of joy; at thy right hand there are pleasures for evermore.

    Acts 2:28 Thou hast made known to me the ways of life; thou shalt make me full of joy with thy countenance.

    2. In sadness and grief.

    Psalm 30:5 For his anger endureth but a moment; in his favour is life: weeping may endure for a night, but joy cometh in the morn-

ing.

Psalm 126:4   Turn again our captivity, O Lord, as the streams in the south.

v.5   They that sow in tears shall reap in joy.

3.   In trouble, lack and barrenness.

Habakkuk 3:16   When I heard, my belly trembled; my lips quivered at the voice: rottenness entered into my bones, and I trembled in myself, that I might rest in the day of trouble: when he cometh up unto the people, he will invade them with his troops.

v.17   Although the fig tree shall not blossom, neither shall fruit be in the vines; the labour of the olive shall fail, and the fields shall yield no meat; the flock shall be cut off from the fold, and there shall be no herd in the stalls:

v.18   Yet I will rejoice in the Lord, I will joy in the God of my salvation.

E.   The joy of the Lord is your strength.

Nehemiah 8:10   Then he said unto them, Go your way, eat the fat, and drink the sweet, and send portions unto them for whom nothing is prepared: for this day is holy unto our Lord: neither be ye sorry; for the joy of the Lord is your strength.

III.   PEACE

A.   From the Greek word *eiro,* which means quietness, rest and, by implication, prosperity.

B.   Peace has been provided by God.

1.   As a blessing.

Psalm 29:11   The Lord will give strength unto his people; the Lord will bless his people with peace.

2.   Through His Son, the Prince of Peace.

John 14:27   Peace I leave with you, my peace I give unto you: not as the world giveth, give I unto you. Let not your heart be troubled,

neither let it be afraid.

3. For encouragement.

    John 16:33 These things I have spoken unto you, that in me ye might have peace. In the world ye shall have tribulation: but be of good cheer; I have overcome the world.

4. For your children.

    Isaiah 54:13 And all thy children shall be taught of the Lord; and great shall be the peace of thy children.

5. For your home.

    Psalm 122:7 Peace be within thy walls, and prosperity within thy palaces.

6. For your attitude.

    Psalm 119:165 Great peace have they which love thy law: and nothing shall offend them.

C. Peace is a covenant.

    Ezekiel 37:26 Moreover I will make a covenant of peace with them; it shall be an everlasting covenant with them: and I will place them, and multiply them, and will set my sanctuary in the midst of them for evermore.

    Malachi 2:5 My covenant was with him of life and peace; and I gave them to him for the fear wherewith he feared me, and was afraid before my name.

D. Peace is a person.

    Ephesians 2:14 For he is our peace, who hath made both one, and hath broken down the middle wall of partition between us.

E. You can have perfect peace.

    Isaiah 26:3 Thou wilt keep him in perfect peace, whose mind is stayed on thee: because he trusteth in thee.

    Philippians 4:7 And the peace of God, which passeth all under-

standing, shall keep your hearts and minds through Christ Jesus.

F.   You can be at peace with others.

> *1 Peter 3:9 Not rendering evil for evil, or railing for railing: but contrariwise blessing; knowing that ye are thereunto called, that ye should inherit a blessing.*
>
> *v.10 For he that will love life, and see good days, let him refrain his tongue from evil, and his lips that they speak no guile:*
>
> *v.11 Let him eschew evil, and do good; let him seek peace, and ensue it.*
>
> *Proverbs 16:7 When a man's ways please the Lord, he maketh even his enemies to be at peace with him.*

IV.   LONGSUFFERING

A.   From the Greek word *makrothuumia*, meaning forbearance and patience.

B.   It is essential in relationships with people.

> *Ephesians 4:2 With all lowliness and meekness, with longsuffering, forbearing one another in love.*
>
> *1 Thessalonians 5:14 Now we exhort you, brethren, warn them that are unruly, comfort the feebleminded, support the weak, be patient toward all men.*
>
> *Colossians 3:12 Put on therefore, as the elect of God, holy and beloved, bowels of mercies, kindness, humbleness of mind, meekness, longsuffering;*
>
> *v.13 Forbearing one another, and forgiving one another, if any man have a quarrel against any: even as Christ forgave you, so also do ye.*

C.   It is essential in waiting for the promises of God.

> *Hebrews 6:15 And so, after he had patiently endured, he obtained the promise.*
>
> *James 5:7 Be patient therefore, brethren, unto the coming of the Lord. Behold, the husbandman waiteth for the precious fruit of the earth, and hath long patience for it, until he receive the early and*

latter rain.

V.   GENTLENESS

    A.   From the Greek word *otos,* meaning excellence in character, and sometimes interchangeable with goodness or kindness.

    B.   Gentleness is demonstrated by God.

> *Luke 6:35 But love ye your enemies, and do good, and lend, hoping for nothing again; and your reward shall be great, and ye shall be the children of the Highest: for he is kind unto the unthankful and to the evil.*

> *Titus 3:4 But after that the kindness and love of God our Saviour toward man appeared.*

    C.   Gentleness promotes character development.

> *2 Corinthians 6:3 Giving no offence in any thing, that the ministry be not blamed:*

> *v.4 But in all things approving ourselves as the ministers of God, in much patience, in afflictions, in necessities, in distresses,*

> *v.5 In stripes, in imprisonments, in tumults, in labours, in watchings, in fastings;*

> *v.6 By pureness, by knowledge, by longsuffering, by kindness, by the Holy Ghost, by love unfeigned.*

    D.   Gentleness is not weak by nature.

> *Romans 15:14 And I myself also am persuaded of you, my brethren, that ye also are full of goodness, filled with all knowledge, able also to admonish one another.*

    E.   Gentleness in simplest terms.

> *Matthew 7:12 Therefore all things whatsoever ye would that men should do to you, do ye even so to them: for this is the law and the prophets.*

VI. GOODNESS

    A.   From the Greek Word *agathosune,* meaning virtue and moral excellence marked by

kind or charitable acts.

B. The preparation for goodness.

> *2 Timothy 2:21 If a man therefore purge himself from these, he shall be a vessel unto honour, sanctified, and meet for the master's use, and prepared unto every good work.*

> *Romans 12:2 And be not conformed to this world: but be ye transformed by the renewing of your mind, that ye may prove what is that good, and acceptable, and perfect, will of God.*

> *Romans 12:9 Let love be without dissimulation. Abhor that which is evil; cleave to that which is good.*

C. The purpose of goodness

1. To overcome evil.

> *Romans 12:21 Be not overcome of evil, but overcome evil with good.*

2. To banish fear of tyranny.

> *Romans 13:3 For rulers are not a terror to good works, but to the evil. Wilt thou then not be afraid of the power? do that which is good, and thou shalt have praise of the same:*

> *v.4 For he is the minister of God to thee for good. But if thou do that which is evil, be afraid; for he beareth not the sword in vain: for he is the minister (servant of the law) of God, a revenger to execute wrath upon him that doeth evil.*

D. The results of goodness.

> *Romans 2:10 But glory, honour, and peace, to every man that worketh good, to the Jew first, and also to the Gentile.*

E. Some examples of goodness.

1. Dorcas

> *Acts 9:36 Now there was at Joppa a certain disciple named Tabitha, which by interpretation is called Dorcas: this woman was full of good works and alms deeds which she did.*

2. Barnabas

> *Acts 11:24 For he was a good man, and full of the Holy Ghost and*

of faith: and much people was added unto the Lord.

VII. FAITH

    A. From the Greek word *pistis,* meaning persuasion, trustworthiness; not to be confused with the gift of faith.

        Hebrews 11:1 Now faith is the substance of things hoped for, the evidence of things not seen.

    B. "A little dab'll do ya."

        Romans 12:3 For I say, through the grace given unto me, to every man that is among you, not to think of himself more highly than he ought to think; but to think soberly, according as God hath dealt to every man the measure of faith.

        Luke 17:6 And the Lord said, If ye had faith as a grain of mustard seed, ye might say unto this sycamine tree, Be thou plucked up by the root, and be thou planted in the sea; and it should obey you.

    C. "Gotta have It."

        Romans 14:23 And he that doubteth is damned if he eat, because he eateth not of faith: for whatsoever is not of faith is sin.

        Galatians 3:14 That the blessing of Abraham might come on the Gentiles through Jesus Christ; that we might receive the promise of the Spirit through faith.

    D. "Don't leave home without it."

        Hebrews 11:6 But without faith it is impossible to please him: for he that cometh to God must believe that he is, and that he is a rewarder of them that diligently seek him.

        2 Corinthians 5:7 For we walk by faith, not by sight.

    E. "Just do it."

        Romans 1:17 For therein is the righteousness of God revealed from faith to faith: as it is written, The just shall live by faith.

    F. "It does a body good."

        Jude 20 But ye, beloved, building up yourselves on your most holy faith, praying in the Holy Ghost.

G. "The best never rest."

Ephesians 6:16 Above all, taking the shield of faith, wherewith ye shall be able to quench all the fiery darts of the wicked.

1 Timothy 6:12 Fight the good fight of faith, lay hold on eternal life, whereunto thou art also called, and hast professed a good profession before many witnesses.

VIII. MEEKNESS

A. From the Greek word *prautes,* meaning mildness and humility; also gentle and submissive to the will of God.

B. Seek meekness.

1 Timothy 6:11 But thou, O man of God, flee these things; and follow after righteousness, godliness, faith, love, patience, meekness.

C. Copy meekness.

Matthew 11:29 Take my yoke upon you, and learn of me; for I am meek and lowly in heart: and ye shall find rest unto your souls.

D. Cherish meekness.

1 Peter 3:4 But let it be the hidden man of the heart, in that which is not corruptible, even the ornament of a meek and quiet spirit, which is in the sight of God of great price.

E. Wear meekness.

Colossians 3:12 Put on therefore, as the elect of God, holy and beloved, bowels of mercies, kindness, humbleness of mind, meekness, longsuffering.

F. Show meekness.

Titus 3:2 To speak evil of no man, to be no brawlers, but gentle, shewing all meekness unto all men.

G. Use meekness.

2 Timothy 2:25 In meekness instructing those that oppose themselves; if God peradventure will give them repentance to the ac-

knowledging of the truth.

H. Restore with meekness.

> *Galatians 6:1 Brethren, if a man be overtaken in a fault, ye which are spiritual, restore such an one in the spirit of meekness; considering thyself, lest thou also be tempted.*

I. Reward of meekness.

> *Matthew 5:5 Blessed are the meek: for they shall inherit the earth.*

IX. TEMPERANCE

A. From the Greek word *egkrateia,* meaning self-control or self-restraint.

B. Imperative for leadership.

> *Titus 1:8 But a lover of hospitality, a lover of good men, sober, just, holy, temperate.*

C. Imperative for men, women, and servants.

> *Titus 2:1 But speak thou the things which become sound doctrine:*
>
> *v.2 That the aged men be sober, grave, temperate, sound in faith, in charity, in patience.*
>
> *v.3 The aged women likewise, that they be in behaviour as becometh holiness, not false accusers, not given to much wine, teachers of good things;*
>
> *v.4 That they may teach the young women to be sober, to love their husbands, to love their children,*
>
> *v.5 To be discreet, chaste, keepers at home, good, obedient to their own husbands, that the word of God be not blasphemed.*
>
> *v.6 Young men likewise exhort to be sober minded.*
>
> *v.7 In all things shewing thyself a pattern of good works: in doctrine shewing uncorruptness, gravity, sincerity,*
>
> *v.8 Sound speech, that cannot be condemned; that he that is of the contrary part may be ashamed, having no evil thing to say of you.*

v.9 Exhort servants to be obedient unto their own masters, and to please them well in all things; not answering again;

v.10 Not purloining, but shewing all good fidelity; that they may adorn the doctrine of God our Saviour in all things.

v.11 For the grace of God that bringeth salvation hath appeared to all men,

v.12 Teaching us that, denying ungodliness and worldly lusts, we should live soberly, righteously, and godly, in this present world.

D. A condition for reward.

1 Corinthians 9:24 Know ye not that they which run in a race run all, but one receiveth the prize? So run, that ye may obtain.

v.25 And every man that striveth for the mastery is temperate in all things. Now they do it to obtain a corruptible crown; but we an incorruptible.

Three:

CHRISTIAN LIVING

COMMUNION

Dear Pastor Parsley:

I have been taking communion in my church, but I am not sure I understand it. I know I am not supposed to have any unconfessed sin in my heart when I take it. Other than that, I don't know why it is such an important thing in my church.

I. INSTITUTED BY THE LORD JESUS CHRIST HIMSELF

> *1 Corinthians 11:23 For I have received of the Lord that which also I delivered unto you, That the Lord Jesus the same night in which he was betrayed took bread:*
>
> *v.24 And when he had given thanks, he brake it, and said, Take, eat: this is my body, which is broken for you: this do in remembrance of me.*
>
> *v.25 After the same manner also he took the cup, when he had supped, saying, This cup is the new testament in my blood: this do ye, as oft as ye drink it, in remembrance of me.*

II. INSTITUTED AS A REMEMBRANCE, NOT A RITUAL

III. FULFILLED THE OLD TESTAMENT TYPE AND SHADOW

A. The Old Testament type of communion was Passover.

B. A commemorative feast celebrated yearly by the Jews in remembrance of their deliverance from Egyptian bondage.

> *Exodus 12:14 And this day shall be unto you for a memorial; and ye shall keep it a feast to the Lord throughout your generations; ye shall keep it a feast by an ordinance for ever.*

C. Two main elements

1.   Flesh of the lamb

Exodus 12:8 And they shall eat the flesh in that night, roast with fire, and unleavened bread; and with bitter herbs they shall eat it.

v.9 Eat not of it raw, nor sodden at all with water, but roast with fire; his head with his legs, and with the purtenance thereof.

2.   Blood of the lamb

Exodus 12:7 And they shall take of the blood, and strike it on the two side posts and on the upper door post of the houses, wherein they shall eat it.

Exodus 12:13 And the blood shall be to you for a token upon the houses where ye are: and when I see the blood, I will pass over you, and the plague shall not be upon you to destroy you, when I smite the land of Egypt.

D.   The New Testament fulfillment is Holy Communion.

1.   A commemorative feast celebrated as often as believers desire, in remembrance of their deliverance from Satanic bondage.

1 Corinthians 11:24 And when he had given thanks, he brake it, and said, Take eat: this is my body, which is broken for you: this do in remembrance of me.

v.25 After the same manner also he took the cup, when he had supped, saying, This cup is the new testament in my blood: this do ye, as oft as ye drink it, in remembrance of me.

2.   Two main elements

1 Corinthians 11:26 For as often as ye eat this bread, and drink this cup, ye do shew the Lord's death till he come.

a.   The body of the Lord (bread) was broken for our physical healing.

b.   The blood of the Lord (fruit of the vine) was shed for the forgiveness of our sin.

IV. SOME IMPORTANT POINTS ABOUT COMMUNION

A. It is a celebration of life, not death.

B. It is for physical healing as well as forgiveness.

C. It can be partaken of as often as desired.

D. The elements of communion are only symbols, not the real thing.

  1. Jesus' literal body is in heaven at the right hand of God.

  Hebrews 10:12 But this man, after he had offered one sacrifice for sins for ever, sat down on the right hand of God;

  v.13 From henceforth expecting till his enemies be made his foot-stool.

  2. His blood has already been applied for the remission of our sins.

  Hebrews 9:22 And almost all things are by the law purged with blood; and without shedding of blood is no remission.

  v.23 It was therefore necessary that the patterns of things in the heavens should be purified with these; but the heavenly things themselves with better sacrifices than these.

E. Believers should examine themselves before partaking.

  1 Corinthians 11:28 But let a man examine himself, and so let him eat of that bread, and drink of that cup.

  v.29 For he that eateth and drinketh unworthily, eateth and drinketh damnation to himself, not discerning the Lord's body.

  v.30 For this cause many are weak and sickly among you, and many sleep [die].

STEWARDSHIP

Dear Pastor Parsley:

My pastor talks a lot about money. I get sick of hearing about it all the time. He calls it "stewardship." Can you tell me what stewardship is and what it has to do with giving money to my church?

I. PRINCIPLES OF STEWARDSHIP

    A. A steward actively directs affairs, a manager.

    B. Stewardship is fulfilling the responsibility of a steward; active and faithful management of that which belongs to another.

    C. We are managers, not owners.

> *Psalms 50:10 For every beast of the forest is mine, and the cattle upon a thousand hills.*

        1. We are the possessors of nothing, but the stewards of everything.

        2. Our very lives do not belong to us.

           a. We are not our own. We have been bought with a price.

> *1 Corinthians 6:19 What? know ye not that your body is the temple of the Holy Ghost which is in you, which ye have of God, and ye are not your own?*

> *v.20 For ye are bought with a price: therefore glorify God in your body, and in your spirit, which are God's.*

           b. The Lord bought (ransomed and redeemed) us from sin and destruction.

        3. We must realize everything in our lives is a result of the mercy of God.

> *James 1:17 Every good gift and every perfect gift is from above, and cometh down from the Father of lights, with whom is no variableness, neither shadow of turning.*

> *John 10:10 The thief cometh not, but for to steal, and to kill, and to destroy: I am come that they might have life, and that they might have it more abundantly.*

Deuteronomy 8:18 But thou shalt remember the Lord thy God: for it is he that giveth thee power to get wealth, that he may establish his covenant which he sware unto thy fathers, as it is this day.

4. We must not allow earthly things to distract our attention from heavenly things.

2 Timothy 2:3 Thou therefore endure hardness, as a good soldier of Jesus Christ.

v.4 No man that warreth entangleth himself with the affairs of this life; that he may please him who hath chosen him to be a soldier.

a. We cannot serve God and man.

Matthew 6:19 Lay not up for yourselves treasures upon earth, where moth and rust doth corrupt, and where thieves break through and steal:

v.20 But lay up for yourselves treasures in heaven, where neither moth nor rust doth corrupt, and where thieves do not break through nor steal:

v.21 For where your treasure is, there will your heart be also.

v.22 The light of the body is the eye: if therefore thine eye be single, thy whole body shall be full of light.

v.23 But if thine eye be evil, thy whole body shall be full of darkness. If therefore the light that is in thee be darkness, how great is that darkness!

v.24 No man can serve two masters: for either he will hate the one, and love the other; or else he will hold to the one, and despise the other. Ye cannot serve God and mammon.

b. Paul left all his earthly credentials behind to follow Jesus.

Philippians 3:3 For we are the circumcision, which worship God in the spirit, and rejoice in Christ Jesus, and have no confidence in the flesh.

v.4 Though I might also have confidence in the flesh. If any other man thinketh that he hath whereof he might trust in the flesh, I more:

v.5 Circumcised the eighth day, of the stock of Israel, of the tribe of Benjamin, an Hebrew of the Hebrews; as touching the law, a Pharisee;

v.6 Concerning zeal, persecuting the church; touching the righteousness which is in the law, blameless.

v.7 But what things were gain to me, those I counted loss for Christ.

v.8 Yea doubtless, and I count all things but loss for the excellency of the knowledge of Christ Jesus my Lord: for whom I have suffered the loss of all things, and do count them but dung, that I may win Christ,

v.9 And be found in him, not having mine own righteousness, which is of the law, but that which is through the faith of Christ, the righteousness which is of God by faith.

c.   Trust in God rather than in riches.

1 Timothy 6:6 But godliness with contentment is great gain.

v.7 For we brought nothing into this world, and it is certain we can carry nothing out.

v.8 And having food and raiment let us be therewith content.

v.9 But they that will be rich fall into temptation and a snare, and into many foolish and hurtful lusts, which drown men in destruction and perdition.

v.10 For the love of money is the root of all evil: which while some coveted after, they have erred from the faith, and pierced themselves through with many sorrows.

1 Tim 6:17 Charge them that are rich in this world, that they be not highminded, nor trust in uncertain riches, but in the living God, who giveth us richly all things to enjoy;

v.18 That they do good, that they be rich in good works, ready to distribute, willing to communicate;

v.19 Laying up in store for themselves a good foundation against the time to come, that they may lay hold on eternal life.

5. God requires certain things of His stewards.

   a. Liberality

   Matthew 10:18 And ye shall be brought before governors and kings for my sake, for a testimony against them and the Gentiles.

   2 Corinthians 9:6 But this I say, He which soweth sparingly shall reap also sparingly; and he which soweth bountifully shall reap also bountifully.

   v.7 Every man according as he purposeth in his heart, so let him give; not grudgingly, or of necessity: for God loveth a cheerful giver.

   b. Faithfulness (trustworthiness)

   1 Corinthians 4:2 Moreover it is required in stewards, that a man be found faithful.

   Luke 16:10 He that is faithful in that which is least is faithful also in much: and he that is unjust in the least is unjust also in much.

   v.11 If therefore ye have not been faithful in the unrighteous mammon, who will commit to your trust the true riches?

   v.12 And if ye have not been faithful in that which is another man's, who shall give you that which is your own?

   Matthew 25:14 For the kingdom of heaven is as a man travelling into a far country, who called his own servants, and delivered unto them his goods.

6. We possess things from God that the world desperately needs.

   a. The mysteries of God.

   1 Corinthians 4:1 Let a man so account of us, as of the ministers of Christ, and stewards of the mysteries of God.

   b. The manifold grace of God.

   1 Peter 4:10 As every man hath received the gift, even so minister the same one to another, as good stewards of the manifold grace of God.

c.   Christ in us, the hope of glory.

Colossians 1:27 To whom God would make known what is the riches of the glory of this mystery among the Gentiles; which is Christ in you, the hope of glory.

II.   TWO MAJOR AREAS OF STEWARDSHIP

A.   We are stewards of our time.

1.   We are to give time to God.

a.   In praise and worship.

Hebrews 13:15 By him therefore let us offer the sacrifice of praise to God continually, that is, the fruit of our lips giving thanks to his name.

b.   In prayer.

Luke 18:1 And he spake a parable unto them to this end, that men ought always to pray, and not to faint.

c.   In Bible reading, study and meditation.

2 Timothy 2:15 Study to shew thyself approved unto God, a workman that needeth not to be ashamed, rightly dividing the word of truth.

2.   We are to give time to others in service or ministry.

Matthew 25:40 And the King shall answer and say unto them, Verily I say unto you, Inasmuch as ye have done it unto one of the least of these my brethren, ye have done it unto me.

B.   We are the stewards of our talents (abilities).

1.   Parable of the talents.

Matthew 25:14 For the kingdom of heaven is as a man travelling into a far country, who called his own servants, and delivered unto them his goods.

v.15 And unto one he gave five talents, to another two, and to another one; to every man according to his several ability; and straightway took his journey.

v.16 Then he that had received the five talents went and traded with the same, and made them other five talents.

v.17 And likewise he that had received two, he also gained other two.

v.18 But he that had received one went and digged in the earth, and hid his lord's money.

v.19 After a long time the lord of those servants cometh, and reckoneth with them.

v.20 And so he that had received five talents came and brought other five talents, saying, Lord, thou deliveredst unto me five talents: behold, I have gained beside them five talents more.

v.21 His lord said unto him, Well done, thou good and faithful servant: thou hast been faithful over a few things, I will make thee ruler over many things: enter thou into the joy of thy lord.

v.22 He also that had received two talents came and said, Lord, thou deliveredst unto me two talents: behold, I have gained two other talents beside them.

v.23 His lord said unto him, Well done, good and faithful servant; thou hast been faithful over a few things, I will make thee ruler over many things: enter thou into the joy of thy lord.

v.24 Then he which had received the one talent came and said, Lord, I knew thee that thou art an hard man, reaping where thou hast not sown, and gathering where thou hast not strawed:

v.25 And I was afraid, and went and hid thy talent in the earth: lo, there thou hast that is thine.

v.26 His lord answered and said unto him, Thou wicked and slothful servant, thou knewest that I reap where I sowed not, and gather where I have not strawed:

v.27 Thou oughtest therefore to have put my money to the exchangers, and then at my coming I should have received mine own with usury.

v.28 Take therefore the talent from him, and give it unto him which hath ten talents.

v.29 For unto every one that hath shall be given, and he shall have abundance: but from him that hath not shall be taken away even that which he hath.

v.30 And cast ye the unprofitable servant into outer darkness: there shall be weeping and gnashing of teeth.

    a. Every servant had some ability.

    b. Some had more than others.

    c. They were not rewarded on the basis of how much they had, but on how well they fulfilled their stewardship.

  2. Natural qualifications are not the same as spiritual qualifications.

    a. God looks on the heart.

1 Samuel 16:7 But the Lord said unto Samuel, Look not on his countenance, or on the height of his stature; because I have refused him: for the Lord seeth not as man seeth; for man looketh on the outward appearance, but the Lord looketh on the heart.

    b. Character is more difficult to develop than talent.

  3. Whatever ability God has given you, use it to its full potential for the glory of God.

C. We are the stewards of our treasure (money).

  1. Giving financially is important.

    a. Financial giving in obedience to God's Word brings blessing.

    b. God has established laws of sowing and reaping.

Mark 4:26 And he said, So is the kingdom of God, as if a man should cast seed into the ground;

v.27 And should sleep, and rise night and day, and the seed should spring and grow up, he knoweth not how.

v.28 For the earth bringeth forth fruit of herself; first the blade, then the ear, after that the full corn in the ear.

v.29 But when the fruit is brought forth, immediately he putteth in the sickle, because the harvest is come.

Mark 10:29 And Jesus answered and said, Verily I say unto you, There is no man that hath left house, or brethren, or sisters, or father, or mother, or wife, or children, or lands, for my sake, and the gospel's,

v.30 But he shall receive an hundredfold now in this time, houses, and brethren, and sisters, and mothers, and children, and lands, with persecutions; and in the world to come eternal life.

Luke 6:38 Give, and it shall be given unto you; good measure, pressed down, and shaken together, and running over, shall men give into your bosom. For with the same measure that ye mete withal it shall be measured to you again.

Galatians 6:7 Be not deceived; God is not mocked: for whatsoever a man soweth, that shall he also reap.

c. We worship with our giving.

Deuteronomy 26:1 And it shall be, when thou art come in unto the land which the Lord thy God giveth thee for an inheritance, and possessest it, and dwellest therein.

v.2 That thou shalt take of the first of all the fruit of the earth, which thou shalt bring of thy land that the Lord thy God giveth thee, and shalt put it in a basket, and shalt go unto the place which the Lord thy God shall choose to place his name there.

d. We finance the Gospel by our giving.

Deuteronomy 8:18 But thou shalt remember the Lord thy God: for it is he that giveth thee power to get wealth, that he may establish his covenant which he sware unto thy fathers, as it is this day.

e. Giving money represents giving ourselves (our money represents our life).

2. Tithing

   a. From the Hebrew word *maasrah,* meaning tenth.

b.   A tenth of our gross (firstfruits), not our net increase.

Genesis 4:3   And in process of time it came to pass, that Cain brought of the fruit of the ground an offering unto the Lord.

v.4   And Abel, he also brought of the firstlings of his flock and of the fat thereof. And the Lord had respect unto Abel and to his offering.

Genesis 14:18   And Melchizedek king of Salem brought forth bread and wine: and he was the priest of the most high God.

v.19   And he blessed him, and said, Blessed be Abram of the most high God, possessor of heaven and earth.

Genesis 28:20   And Jacob vowed a vow, saying, If God will be with me, and will keep me in this way that I go, and will give me bread to eat, and raiment to put on,

v.21   So that I come again to my father's house in peace; then shall the Lord be my God:

v.22   And this stone, which I have set for a pillar, shall be God's house: and of all that thou shalt give me I will surely give the tenth unto thee.

Deuteronomy 26:2   That thou shalt take of the first of all the fruit of the earth, which thou shalt bring of thy land that the Lord thy God giveth thee, and shalt put it in a basket, and shalt go unto the place which the Lord thy God shall choose to place his name there.

c.   We bring the tithe to the priest in his office.

   1)   In the Old Testament, the priest was a man.

Deuteronomy 26:3   And thou shalt go unto the priest that shall be in those days, and say unto him, I profess this day unto the Lord thy God, that I am come unto the country which the Lord sware unto our fathers for to give us.

v.4   And the priest shall take the basket out of thine hand, and set it down before the altar of the Lord thy God.

2)   In the New Testament, the priest is Jesus Christ.

Hebrews 7:5   And verily they that are of the sons of Levi, who receive the office of the priesthood, have a commandment to take tithes of the people according to the law, that is, of their brethren, though they come out of the loins of Abraham:

v.6   But he whose descent is not counted from them received tithes of Abraham, and blessed him that had the promises.

v.7   And without all contradiction the less is blessed of the better.

v.8   And here men that die receive tithes; but there he receiveth them, of whom it is witnessed that he liveth.

d.   Bring your tithe into the storehouse where you receive spiritual food.

Malachi 3:10   Bring ye all the tithes into the storehouse, that there may be meat in mine house, and prove me now herewith, saith the Lord of hosts, if I will not open you the windows of heaven, and pour you out a blessing, that there shall not be room enough to receive it.

e.   Make your confession of faith when you bring your tithe.

Deuteronomy 26:3   And thou shalt go unto the priest that shall be in those days, and say unto him, I profess this day unto the Lord thy God, that I am come unto the country which the Lord sware unto our fathers for to give us.

Deuteronomy 26:5   And thou shalt speak and say before the Lord thy God, A Syrian ready to perish was my father, and he went down into Egypt, and sojourned there with a few, and became there a nation, great, mighty, and populous:

v.6   And the Egyptians evil entreated us, and afflicted us, and laid upon us hard bondage:

v.7   And when we cried unto the Lord God of our fathers, the Lord heard our voice, and looked on our affliction, and our labour, and our oppression:

v.8   And the Lord brought us forth out of Egypt with a mighty hand, and with an outstretched arm, and with great terribleness, and with signs, and with wonders:

v.9   And he hath brought us into this place, and hath given us this

land, even a land that floweth with milk and honey.

v.10   And now, behold, I have brought the firstfruits of the land, which thou, O Lord, hast given me. And thou shalt set it before the Lord thy God, and worship before the Lord thy God:

v.11   And thou shalt rejoice in every good thing which the Lord thy God hath given unto thee, and unto thine house, thou, and the Levite, and the stranger that is among you.

3.   Offerings

    a.   Offerings are above and beyond tithing.

    b.   Offerings can be for different purposes.

        1)   To spread the Gospel.

        2)   To minister to the poor.

        3)   As a praise to God.

        4)   As a sacrifice.

        5)   Simply because you want to.

4.   Areas to avoid in giving

    a.   Giving where God has not placed His name.

Deuteronomy 26:2   That thou shalt take of the first of all the fruit of the earth, which thou shalt bring of thy land that the Lord thy God giveth thee, and shalt put it in a basket, and shalt go unto the place which the Lord thy God shall choose to place his name there.

    b.   Giving for an unclean use or for the dead.

Deuteronomy 26:14   I have not eaten thereof in my mourning, neither have I taken away ought thereof for any unclean use, nor given ought thereof for the dead: but I have hearkened to the voice of the Lord my God, and have done according to all that thou hast commanded me.

    c.   Giving grudgingly or of necessity.

2 Corinthians 9:7   Every man according as he purposeth in his heart, so let him give; not grudgingly, or of necessity: for God loveth

a cheerful giver.

d.   Withholding tithes or offerings.

    1)   A tithe withheld must be paid with 20% interest added.

Leviticus 27:31 And if a man will at all redeem ought of his tithes, he shall add thereto the fifth part thereof.

    2)   It tends to poverty.

Proverbs 11:24 There is that scattereth, and yet increaseth; and there is that withholdeth more than is meet, but it tendeth to poverty.

e.   Robbing God.

Malachi 3:8 Will a man rob God? Yet ye have robbed me. But ye say, Wherein have we robbed thee? In tithes and offerings.

v.9 Ye are cursed with a curse: for ye have robbed me, even this whole nation.

PRAYER

Dear Pastor Parsley:

I have been praying a long time for God to do something for me. I sometimes think God doesn't care. Can you tell me how to pray so God will hear me?

I.   SIX STEPS TO ANSWERED PRAYER.

> *2 Chronicles 7:14 If my people, which are called by my name, shall humble themselves, and pray, and seek my face, and turn from their wicked ways; then will I hear from heaven, and will forgive their sin, and will heal their land.*

> *Ephesians 6:18 Praying always with all prayer and supplication in the Spirit, and watching thereunto with all perseverance and supplication for all saints.*

A.   Decide specifically what you want from God.

> *Philemon 6 That the communication of thy faith may become effectual by the acknowledging of every good thing which is in you in Christ Jesus.*

B.   Know God's will.

1.   God's Word is His will.

2.   The Holy Spirit will reveal God's will.

C.   Ask what you want from God.

> *Luke 11:9 And I say unto you, Ask, and it shall be given you; seek, and ye shall find; knock, and it shall be opened unto you.*

> *Philippians 4:6 Be careful for nothing; but in every thing by prayer and supplication with thanksgiving let your requests be made known unto God.*

> *1 John 5:14 And this is the confidence that we have in him, that, if we ask any thing according to his will, he heareth us:*

> *v.15 And if we know that he hear us, whatsoever we ask, we know that we have the petitions that we desired of him.*

1. Ask with confidence.

2. Ask in faith, believing.

D. Refuse doubt.

> *2 Corinthians 10:15 Not boasting of things without our measure, that is, of other men's labours; but having hope, when your faith is increased, that we shall be enlarged by you according to our rule abundantly.*

1. Doubt is of the devil.

2. Replace doubt with faith.

E. Bind and loose.

> *Matthew 16:19 And I will give unto thee the keys of the kingdom of heaven: and whatsoever thou shalt bind on earth shall be bound in heaven: and whatsoever thou shalt loose on earth shall be loosed in heaven.*

F. Begin to praise.

> *Hebrews 13:15 By him therefore let us offer the sacrifice of praise to God continually, that is, the fruit of our lips giving thanks to his name.*

II. WHAT IS PRAYER?

A. Communing and conversing with, asking and receiving from God.

B. Prayer involves:

1. Supplication, making requests of God.

2. Declaration, informing principalities and powers in the spirit realm of two things in your life.

    a. The Kingdom of God being accomplished.

    b. The will of God being done.

III. DIFFERENT KINDS OF PRAYER

A. Prayer of Authority or Prayer of Binding and Loosing

Matthew 16:19 And I will give unto thee the keys of the kingdom of heaven: and whatsoever thou shalt bind on earth shall be bound in heaven: and whatsoever thou shalt loose on earth shall be loosed in heaven.

Psalm 2:7 I will declare the decree: the Lord hath said unto me, Thou art my Son; this day have I begotten thee.

B. Prayer of Agreement

Matthew 18:19 Again I say unto you, That if two of you shall agree on earth as touching any thing that they shall ask, it shall be done for them of my Father which is in heaven.

Acts 4:31 And when they had prayed, the place was shaken where they were assembled together; and they were all filled with the Holy Ghost, and they spake the word of God with boldness.

C. Prayer of Petition or Faith

Mark 11:22 And Jesus answering saith unto them, Have faith in God.

v.23 For verily I say unto you, That whosoever shall say unto this mountain, Be thou removed, and be thou cast into the sea; and shall not doubt in his heart, but shall believe that those things which he saith shall come to pass; he shall have whatsoever he saith.

v.24 Therefore I say unto you, What things soever ye desire, when ye pray, believe that ye receive them, and ye shall have them.

Matthew 21:21 Jesus answered and said unto them, Verily I say unto you, If ye have faith, and doubt not, ye shall not only do this which is done to the fig tree, but also if ye shall say unto this mountain, Be thou removed, and be thou cast into the sea; it shall be done.

v.22 And all things, whatsoever ye shall ask in prayer, believing, ye shall receive.

D. Prayer of Worship, Thanksgiving or Praise

2 Chronicles 20:18 And Jehoshaphat bowed his head with his face to the ground: and all Judah and the inhabitants of Jerusalem fell before the Lord, worshipping the Lord.

v.19 And the Levites, of the children of the Kohathites, and of the children of the Korhites, stood up to praise the Lord God of Israel with a loud voice on high.

v.20 And they rose early in the morning, and went forth into the wilderness of Tekoa: and as they went forth, Jehoshaphat stood and said, Hear me, O Judah, and ye inhabitants of Jerusalem; Believe in the Lord your God, so shall ye be established; believe his prophets, so shall ye prosper.

v.21 And when he had consulted with the people, he appointed singers unto the Lord and that should praise the beauty of holiness, as they went out before the army, and to say, Praise the Lord; for his mercy endureth for ever.

v.22 And when they began to sing and to praise, the Lord set ambushments against the children of Ammon, Moab, and mount Seir, which were come against Judah; and they were smitten.

Luke 24:52 And they worshipped him, and returned to Jerusalem with great joy:

v.53 And were continually in the temple, praising and blessing God. Amen.

E. Prayer of Commitment, Dedication and Consecration

1. Commitment

Philippians 4:6 Be careful for nothing; but in every thing by prayer and supplication with thanksgiving let your requests be made known unto God.

2. Dedication and consecration

Matthew 26:39 And he went a little further, and fell on his face, and prayed, saying, O my Father, if it be possible, let this cup pass from me: nevertheless not as I will, but as thou wilt.

F. Prayer of Intercession, on Behalf of Another

Isaiah 59:16 And he saw that there was no man, and wondered that there was no intercessor: therefore his arm brought salvation unto him; and his righteousness, it sustained him.

Romans 8:26 Likewise the Spirit also helpeth our infirmities: for we know not what we should pray for as we ought: but the Spirit itself maketh intercession for us with groanings which cannot be uttered.

v.27 And he that searcheth the hearts knoweth what is the mind of the Spirit, because he maketh intercession for the saints according to the will of God.

G. Prayer in the Spirit or in other Tongues

1 Corinthians 14:2 For if I pray in an unknown tongue, my spirit prayeth, but my understanding is unfruitful.

1 Corinthians 14:4 He that speaketh in an unknown tongue edifieth himself; but he that prophesieth edifieth the church.

1 Corinthians 14:14 For if I pray in an unknown tongue, my spirit prayeth, but my understanding is unfruitful.

Jude 20 But ye, beloved, building up yourselves on your most holy faith, praying in the Holy Ghost.

WITNESSING

Dear Pastor Parsley:

I have been saved for two years, and I have a brand new life. I know that part of the Great Commission is that we are to be witnesses. I want to tell people about Jesus, but I just don't feel qualified. I am a very quiet person. Is there some special teaching that would help a shy person like me to become a witness?

I. THE GREAT COMMISSION IS TO SPREAD THE GOSPEL.

> *Matthew 28:18 And Jesus came and spake unto them, saying, All power is given unto me in heaven and in earth.*
>
> *v.19 Go ye therefore, and teach all nations, baptizing them in the name of the Father, and of the Son, and of the Holy Ghost:*
>
> *v.20 Teaching them to observe all things whatsoever I have commanded you: and, lo, I am with you alway, even unto the end of the world. Amen.*
>
> *Mark 16:15 And he said unto them, Go ye into all the world, and preach the gospel to every creature.*
>
> *Luke 24:47 And that repentance and remission of sins should be preached in his name among all nations, beginning at Jerusalem.*

II. THE GREATEST OBSTACLE IS FEAR.

   A. Of rejection

   B. Of people

   C. Of what might go wrong

   D. Of offending someone

III. WE CAN OVERCOME FEAR.

> *2 Timothy 1:7 For God hath not given us the spirit of fear; but of power, and of love, and of a sound mind.*

1 John 4:18 There is no fear in love; but perfect love casteth out fear: because fear hath torment. He that feareth is not made perfect in love.

A. Bind and rebuke fear.

B. Be prepared.

> *1 Peter 3:15 But sanctify the Lord God in your hearts: and be ready always to give an answer to every man that asketh you a reason of the hope that is in you with neekness and fear.*

C. Practice your testimony.

    1. Keep it simple.

    2. Tell them how they can be saved.

D. Pray.

E. Don't be discouraged by rejection.

> *Matthew 10:40 He that receiveth you receiveth me, and he that receiveth me receiveth him that sent me.*

IV. QUALIFICATIONS

A. We are called to be witnesses.

    1. What is a witness?

        a. Someone who gives testimony of what he has seen and heard.

> *Acts 4:20 For we cannot but speak the things which we have seen and heard.*

        b. Someone who produces proof that what he is saying is true.

> *Acts 1:8 But ye shall receive power, after that the Holy Ghost is come upon you: and ye shall be witnesses unto me both in Jerusalem, and in all Judaea, and in Samaria, and unto the uttermost part of the earth.*

    2. A witness is not just someone who is "called to preach," but includes everyone.

3. God wants to use you, one-on-one, with others.

B. We are born of the Spirit.

> *John 3:3 Jesus answered and said unto him, Verily, verily, I say unto thee, Except a man be born again, he cannot see the kingdom of God.*

> *2 Corinthians 5:17 Therefore if any man be in Christ, he is a new creature: old things are passed away; behold, all things are become new.*

C. We are empowered by the Spirit.

> *Luke 24:49 And, behold, I send the promise of my Father upon you: but tarry ye in the city of Jerusalem, until ye be endued with power from on high.*

> *Acts 1:8 But ye shall receive power, after that the Holy Ghost is come upon you: and ye shall be witnesses unto me both in Jerusalem, and in all Judaea, and in Samaria, and unto the uttermost part of the earth.*

D. We have divine assistance.

1. Boldness

> *Acts 4:29 And now, Lord, behold their threatenings: and grant unto thy servants, that with all boldness they may speak thy word.*

> *Ephesians 6:19 And for me, that utterance may be given unto me, that I may open my mouth boldly, to make known the mystery of the gospel.*

2. Opportunity

> *Colossians 4:3 Withal praying also for us, that God would open unto us a door of utterance, to speak the mystery of Christ, for which I am also in bonds.*

> *2 Thessalonians 3:1 Finally, brethren, pray for us, that the word of the Lord may have free course, and be glorified, even as it is with you.*

3. Conviction

John 16:8 And when he is come, he will reprove the world of sin, and of righteousness, and of judgment.

4. Help

1 Corinthians 3:7 So then neither is he that planteth any thing, neither he that watereth; but God that giveth the increase.

V. HOW TO DO IT

A. Speak God's Word.

John 6:63 It is the spirit that quickeneth; the flesh profiteth nothing: the words that I speak unto you, they are spirit, and they are life.

B. Present the Gospel.

1. You can tell your own personal testimony better than anyone else can.

2. No one can challenge your authority about your own life.

C. Work God's works.

John 14:12 Verily, verily, I say unto you, He that believeth on me, the works that I do shall he do also; and greater works than these shall he do; because I go unto my Father.

D. Live a Godly life.

Galatians 2:20 I am crucified with Christ: nevertheless I live; yet not I, but Christ liveth in me: and the life which I now live in the flesh I live by the faith of the Son of God, who loved me, and gave himself for me.

FELLOWSHIP

Dear Pastor Parsley:

My family has been hurt badly because of a recent church split. We feel like we can't trust Christians anymore. We want to have our own church at home. Is it really important that we fellowship at a church?

I. WHAT IS FELLOWSHIP?

    A. From the Greek word *koinonia*, meaning partnership, participation in a social dealing, communication, communion.

    B. Two fellows in the same ship.

II. VERTICAL FELLOWSHIP.

> *1 John 1:3 That which we have seen and heard declare we unto you, that ye also may have fellowship with us: and truly our fellowship is with the Father, and with his Son Jesus Christ.*

    A. Fellowship with the Father.

        1. It is first and foremost.

        2. All other relationships depend on your relationship with Him.

        3. God's entire purpose in redemption is to restore men to a place of fellowship with God.

    B. How do you have fellowship with God?

        1. Bible reading

        2. Scripture study

        3. Meditation on God's Word

        4. Prayer

        5. Praise

        6. Worship

III. HORIZONTAL FELLOWSHIP.

> *1 John 1:7 But if we walk in the light, as he is in the light, we have fellowship one with another, and the blood of Jesus Christ his Son cleanseth us from all sin.*

A. Who participates?

   1. Natural family

      a. Husband and wife

      b. Other family members

   2. Spiritual family

      a. Local body of believers

      b. Entire body of Christ

B. The focal point of fellowship with other believers is the local church.

   1. Believers are commanded to assemble together.

> *Hebrews 10:25 Not forsaking the assembling of ourselves together, as the manner of some is; but exhorting one another: and so much the more, as ye see the day approaching.*

   2. Believers are individual members of a larger body and must find their place in the body and function there to be fulfilled.

> *1 Corinthians 12:27 Now ye are the body of Christ, and members in particular.*

   3. More can be accomplished corporately than individually.

      a. One chases a thousand.

> *Deuteronomy 32:30 How should one chase a thousand, and two put ten thousand to flight, except their Rock had sold them, and the Lord had shut them up?*

      b. Two puts ten thousand to flight (Deuteronomy 32:30).

4.   There is greater safety in numbers.

1 Corinthians 5:11 But now I have written unto you not to keep company, if any man that is called a brother be a fornicator, or covetous, or an idolater, or a railer, or a drunkard, or an extortioner; with such an one no not to eat.

v.12 For what have I to do to judge them also that are without? do not ye judge them that are within?

v.13 But them that are without God judgeth. Therefore put away from among yourselves that wicked person.

Four:

TOUGH ISSUES

SOCIAL DRINKING

Dear Pastor Parsley:

I am in the military, and I am stationed in a remote area. There isn't much to do here on our off time. I am a Christian, but I was just wondering if it would be wrong to go out drinking with my buddies once in a while?

Dear Pastor Parsley:

I am a newlywed, and I don't have any Christian family members I can ask for advice. My new husband just got a terrific promotion, and his boss is having a dinner party to celebrate. I am sure that alcohol will be served at the party. What should we do? Is it wrong to have a drink with dinner?

I. YOUR BODY IS THE DWELLING PLACE OF GOD.

> *1 Corinthians 6:19 What? know ye not that your body is the temple of the Holy Ghost which is in you, which ye have of God, and ye are not your own?*

> *Hosea 4:11 Whoredom and wine and new wine take away the heart.*

II. DRUNKENNESS IS A SIN.

> *Proverbs 31:4 It is not for kings, O Lemuel, it is not for kings to drink wine; nor for princes strong drink.*

> *Revelation 5:10 And hast made us unto our God kings and priests: and we shall reign on the earth.*

> *Proverbs 20:1 Wine is a mocker, strong drink is raging: and whosoever is deceived thereby is not wise.*

> *Proverbs 23:31 Look not thou upon the wine when it is red, when it giveth his colour in the cup, when it moveth itself aright.*

> *v.32 At the last it biteth like a serpent, and stingeth like an adder.*

> *v.33 Thine eyes shall behold strange women, and thine heart shall utter perverse things.*

Ephesians 5:18 And be not drunk with wine, wherein is excess; but be filled with the Spirit.

Habakkuk 2:15 Woe unto him that giveth his neighbour drink, that puttest thy bottle to him, and makest him drunken also, that thou mayest look on their nakedness!

James 4:17 Therefore to him that knoweth to do good, and doeth it not, to him it is sin.

III. THE ENEMY WISHES TO DESTROY THE CHILDREN OF GOD.

Ephesians 4:27 Neither give place to the devil.

1 Peter 5:8 Be sober, be vigilant; because your adversary the devil, as a roaring lion, walketh about, seeking whom he may devour:

v.9 Whom resist stedfast in the faith, knowing that the same afflictions are accomplished in your brethren that are in the world.

IV. THE BIBLE GIVES US GUIDELINES FOR BEHAVIOR.

2 Corinthians 6:17 Wherefore come out from among them, and be ye separate saith the Lord, and touch not the unclean thing; and I will receive you.

Colossians 3:23 And whatsoever ye do, do it heartily, as to the Lord, and not unto men.

1 Thessalonians 5:22 Abstain from all appearance of evil.

HEALING, IS IT FOR TODAY?

Dear Pastor Parsley:

On your *Breakthrough* TV program I watch you pray for people who need healing. I am scheduled to have surgery and the doctors cannot guarantee that it will save my life. My church teaches that miracles were only for Bible times. I know I need a miracle. Please tell me why you believe in praying for the sick in this day and age.

I. JESUS COMMANDS US TO DO IT.

> *Matthew 10:7 And as ye go, preach, saying, The kingdom of heaven is at hand.*
>
> *v.8 Heal the sick, cleanse the lepers, raise the dead, cast out devils: freely ye have received, freely give.*
>
> *Mark 16:15 And he said unto them, Go ye into all the world, and preach the gospel to every creature.*
>
> *v.16 He that believeth and is baptized shall be saved; but he that believeth not shall be damned.*
>
> *v.17 And these signs shall follow them that believe; In my name shall they cast out devils; they shall speak with new tongues;*
>
> *v.18 They shall take up serpents; and if they drink any deadly thing, it shall not hurt them; they shall lay hands on the sick, and they shall recover.*
>
> *v.19 So then after the Lord had spoken unto them, he was received up into heaven, and sat on the right hand of God.*
>
> *v.20 And they went forth, and preached every where, the Lord working with them, and confirming the word with signs following.*

II. WE HAVE POWER OF ATTORNEY.

> *John 14:12 Verily, verily, I say unto you, He that believeth on me, the works that I do shall he do also; and greater works than these shall he do; because I go unto my Father.*
>
> *v.13 And whatsoever ye shall ask in my name, that will I do, that the Father may be glorified in the Son.*

III. GOD PROVIDED FOR IT.

> *Isaiah 53:5 But he was wounded for our transgressions, he was bruised for our iniquities: the chastisement of our peace was upon him; and with his stripes we are healed.*
>
> *2 Chronicles 7:14 If my people, which are called by my name, shall humble themselves, and pray, and seek my face, and turn from their wicked ways; then will I hear from heaven, and will forgive their sin, and will heal their land.*
>
> *Psalm 147:3 He healeth the broken in heart, and bindeth up their wounds.*
>
> *Psalm 103:3 Who forgiveth all thine iniquities; who healeth all thy diseases.*

FORGIVENESS

Dear Pastor Parsley:

When I was a young girl living at home I was sexually abused by my father. He is a prominent man, and I knew no one would believe me if I told them about it. I feel such hatred every time he gets some award for being such a great citizen or when someone tells me how lucky I am to have such a "great father." I have been unable to trust men. Sometimes I am so overcome with bitterness that I suspect all men of being abusers. I don't know why I cannot get free of these feelings that constantly poison my mind.

I. FORGIVENESS IS THE KEY AND IS A COMMAND.

> *Mark 11:25 And when ye stand praying, forgive, if ye have ought against any: that your Father also which is in heaven may forgive you your trespasses.*

> *v.26 But if ye do not forgive, neither will your Father which is in heaven forgive your trespasses.*

> *Ephesians 4:32 And be ye kind one to another, tenderhearted, forgiving one another, even as God for Christ's sake hath forgiven you.*

II. FORGIVENESS TOWARD OTHERS IS NECESSARY IN ORDER TO RECEIVE GOD'S FORGIVENESS.

> *Matthew 18:14 Even so it is not the will of your Father which is in heaven, that one of these little ones should perish.*

> *v.15 Moreover if thy brother shall trespass against thee, go and tell him his fault between thee and him alone: if he shall hear thee, thou hast gained thy brother.*

III. UNFORGIVENESS IS A SIN AND SEPARATES US FROM GOD.

> *James 4:17 Therefore to him that knoweth to do good, and doeth it not, to him it is sin.*

IV. UNFORGIVENESS GIVES SATAN THE ADVANTAGE.

> *2 Corinthians 2:9 For to this end also did I write, that I might know the proof of you, whether ye be obedient in all things.*

v.10 To whom ye forgive any thing, I forgive also: for if I forgave any thing, to whom I forgave it, for your sakes forgave I it in the person of Christ.

1 Peter 5:8 Be sober, be vigilant; because your adversary the devil, as a roaring lion, walketh about, seeking whom he may devour.

James 4:7 Submit yourselves therefore to God. Resist the devil, and he will flee from you.

HOMOSEXUALITY

Dear Pastor Parsley:

I am in a homosexual relationship and both of us are Christians. I believe that God understands because He made us this way. We cannot find a church that accepts us. Doesn't the Bible say we are not to judge each other?

I.   YOUR BODY BELONGS TO GOD.

> *1 Corinthians 6:15 Know ye not that your bodies are the members of Christ? shall I then take the members of Christ, and make them the members of an harlot? God forbid.*
>
> *v.16 What? know ye not that he which is joined to an harlot is one body? for two, saith he, shall be one flesh.*
>
> *v.17 But he that is joined unto the Lord is one spirit.*
>
> *v.18 Flee fornication. Every sin that a man doeth is without the body; but he that committeth fornication sinneth against his own body.*
>
> *v.19 What? know ye not that your body is the temple of the Holy Ghost which is in you, which ye have of God, and ye are not your own?*
>
> *v.20 For ye are bought with a price: therefore glorify God in your body, and in your spirit, which are God's.*

II.   YOU WERE CREATED IN HIS IMAGE.

> *Genesis 1:26 And God said, Let us make man in our image, after our likeness: and let them have dominion over the fish of the sea, and over the fowl of the air, and over the cattle, and over all the earth, and over every creeping thing that creepeth upon the earth.*
>
> *v.27 So God created man in his own image, in the image of God created he him; male and female created he them.*

III. HOMOSEXUALITY IS A SIN.

A. Old Testament

Leviticus 18:22 Thou shalt not lie with mankind, as with woman-kind: it is abomination.

1. Sodomy is considered to be any sexual practice of a nature other than normal sexual intercourse between a man and a woman; covers lesbianism as well as homosexuality and bestiality; also covers heterosexual practices that fall outside the parameters of "normal."

2. Sodom was destroyed because of sexual perversion.

   Genesis 18:20 And the Lord said, Because the cry of Sodom and Gomorrah is great, and because their sin is very grievous;

   v.21 I will go down now, and see whether they have done altogether according to the cry of it, which is come unto me; and if not, I will know.

   Genesis 19:24 Then the Lord rained upon Sodom and upon Gomorrah brimstone and fire from the Lord out of heaven;

   v.25 And he overthrew those cities, and all the plain, and all the inhabitants of the cities, and that which grew upon the ground.

3. Isaiah's Warning.

   Isaiah 3:8 For Jerusalem is ruined, and Judah is fallen: because their tongue and their doings are against the LORD, to provoke the eyes of his glory.

   v.9 The shew of their countenance doth witness against them; and they declare their sin as Sodom, they hide it not. Woe unto their soul! for they have rewarded evil unto themselves.

B. New Testament

1 Corinthians 6:9 Know ye not that the unrighteous shall not inherit the kingdom of God? Be not deceived: neither fornicators, nor idolaters, nor adulterers, nor effeminate, nor abusers of themselves with mankind,

v.10 Nor thieves, nor covetous, nor drunkards, nor revilers, nor extortioners, shall inherit the kingdom of God.

1. Fornication is any sexual relationship outside the marriage relationship between a husband and wife, including adultery and incest.

   Hebrews 13:4 Marriage (as God ordained between a man and a woman) is honourable in all, and the bed undefiled: but whoremongers and adulterers God will judge.

2. From the greek word *arsenokoites*, meaning one guilty of unnatural offenses; sodomite; homosexual; sexual pervert.

   1 Timothy 1:9 Knowing this, that the law is not made for a righteous man, but for the lawless and disobedient, for the ungodly and for sinners, for unholy and profane, for murderers of fathers and murderers of mothers, for manslayers,

   v.10 For whoremongers, for them that defile themselves with mankind, for menstealers, for liars, for perjured persons, and if there be any other thing that is contrary to sound doctrine.

ABORTION

Dear Pastor Parsley:

I am sick and tired of church people getting involved in the abortion issue. It is a matter of personal choice and the church should stay out of it. Abortion is not mentioned in the Bible, so how can the church take it so personally?

I. ABORTION IS A SPIRITUAL ISSUE.

> *Deuteronomy 30:19 I call heaven and earth to record this day against you, that I have set before you life and death, blessing and cursing: therefore choose life, that both thou and thy seed may live.*

> *Ephesians 6:12 For we wrestle not against flesh and blood, but against principalities, against powers, against the rulers of the darkness of this world, against spiritual wickedness in high places.*

II. ABORTION IS SATAN'S ATTEMPT TO DESTROY RIGHTEOUS SEED.

A. It happened in the Old Testament through Pharaoh.

> *Exodus 1:16 And he said, When ye do the office of a midwife to the Hebrew women, and see them upon the stools; if it be a son, then ye shall kill him: but if it be a daughter, then she shall live.*

B. It happened in the New Testament through Herod.

> *Matthew 2:16 Then Herod, when he saw that he was mocked of the wise men, was exceeding wroth, and sent forth, and slew all the children that were in Bethlehem, and in all the coasts thereof, from two years old and under, according to the time which he had diligently inquired of the wise men.*

III. WE ARE TO DEFEND THE CAUSE OF THE HELPLESS.

> *Psalm 82:3 Defend the poor and fatherless: do justice to the afflicted and needy.*

> *v.4 Deliver the poor and needy: rid them out of the hand of the wicked.*

Proverbs 31:8 Open thy mouth for the dumb in the cause of all such as are appointed to destruction.

v.9 Open thy mouth, judge righteously, and plead the cause of the poor and needy.

IV. CHILDREN ARE PRECIOUS TO GOD.

Isaiah 44:24 Thus saith the Lord, thy redeemer, and he that formed thee from the womb, I am the Lord that maketh all things; that stretcheth forth the heavens alone; that spreadeth abroad the earth by myself;

Isaiah 49:1 Listen, O isles, unto me; and hearken, ye people, from far; The Lord hath called me from the womb; from the bowels of my mother hath he made mention of my name.

Psalm 127:3 Lo, children are an heritage of the Lord: and the fruit of the womb is his reward.

Jeremiah 1:5 Before I formed thee in the belly I knew thee; and before thou camest forth out of the womb I sanctified thee, and I ordained thee a prophet unto the nations.

V. THOU SHALT NOT KILL.

Exodus 21:13 And if a man lie not in wait, but God deliver him into his hand; then I will appoint thee a place whither he shall flee.

Genesis 9:6 Whoso sheddeth man's blood, by man shall his blood be shed: for in the image of God made he man.

Deuteronomy 27:25 Cursed be he that taketh reward to slay an innocent person. And all the people shall say, Amen.

Exodus 23:7 Keep thee far from a false matter; and the innocent and righteous slay thou not: for I will not justify the wicked.

Amos 1:13 Thus saith the Lord; For three transgressions of the children of Ammon, and for four, I will not turn away the punishment thereof; because they have ripped up the women with child of Gilead, that they might enlarge their border.

PORNOGRAPHY

Dear Pastor Parsley:

My brother is addicted to pornography. He says he is not a pervert — and there is nothing wrong with it — because he is just looking. Is there anything in the Bible that might help me convince him what he is doing is wrong?

I.   THE WORKS OF THE FLESH

> *Galatians 5:19 Now the works of the flesh are manifest, which are these; Adultery, fornication, uncleanness, lasciviousness,*
>
> *v.20 Idolatry, witchcraft, hatred, variance, emulations, wrath, strife, seditions, heresies,*
>
> *v.21 Envyings, murders, drunkenness, revellings, and such like: of the which I tell you before, as I have also told you in time past, that they which do such things shall not inherit the kingdom of God.*

A.   Fornication includes any sexual gratification outside the bounds of lawful marriage.

1.   Viewing pictures

2.   Reading stimulating materials

3.   Sexual fantasies

B.   Lasciviousness comes from the Greek word *aselgeia*, meaning wantonness, lewd, lustful; tending to arouse sexual desire.

II.   GOD'S PENALTY

> *Jude 1:4 For there are certain men crept in unawares, who were before of old ordained to this condemnation, ungodly men, turning the grace of our God into lasciviousness, and denying the only Lord God, and our Lord Jesus Christ.*
>
> *v.5 I will therefore put you in remembrance, though ye once knew this, how that the Lord, having saved the people out of the land of Egypt, afterward destroyed them that believed not.*

v.6 And the angels which kept not their first estate, but left their own habitation, he hath reserved in everlasting chains under darkness unto the judgment of the great day.

v.7 Even as Sodom and Gomorrha, and the cities about them in like manner, giving themselves over to fornication, and going after strange flesh, are set forth for an example, suffering the vengeance of eternal fire.

v.8 Likewise also these filthy dreamers defile the flesh, despise dominion, and speak evil of dignities.

Ephesians 5:3 But fornication, and all uncleanness, or covetousness, let it not be once named among you, as becometh saints;

v.4 Neither filthiness, nor foolish talking, nor jesting, which are not convenient: but rather giving of thanks.

v.5 For this ye know, that no whoremonger, nor unclean person, nor covetous man, who is an idolater, hath any inheritance in the kingdom of Christ and of God.

v.6 Let no man deceive you with vain words: for because of these things cometh the wrath of God upon the children of disobedience.

v.7 Be not ye therefore partakers with them.

MURDER VS. KILLING IN WARTIME

Dear Pastor Parsley:

In the Ten Commandments it says, "Thou shalt not kill." Can you explain to me why that Scripture is in the Bible when God told the children of Israel to fight so many times and to destroy their enemies?

I.   OLD TESTAMENT

    A. The word translated *kills* in the Old Testament was *ratsach,* meaning literally "to murder."

        Exodus 20:13 Thou shalt not kill.

    B. Any death in keeping with God's Word and sanctioned by the government is not defined as murder.

        Exodus 21:12 He that smiteth a man, so that he die, shall be surely put to death.

        Genesis 9:6 Whoso sheddeth man's blood, by man shall his blood be shed: for in the image of God made he man.

II. OLD TESTAMENT RULES OF WAR

    A. Excused from military duty

       1. In hardship cases

          Deuteronomy 20:5 And the officers shall speak unto the people, saying, What man is there that hath built a new house, and hath not dedicated it? let him go and return to his house, lest he die in the battle, and another man dedicate it.

          v.6 And what man is he that hath planted a vineyard, and hath not yet eaten of it? let him also go and return unto his house, lest he die in the battle, and another man eat of it.

          v.7 And what man is there that hath betrothed a wife, and hath not taken her? let him go and return unto his house, lest he die in the battle, and another man take her.

2. Because of fear

> *Deuteronomy 20:8 And the officers shall speak further unto the people, and they shall say, What man is there that is fearful and fainthearted? let him go and return unto his house, lest his brethren's heart faint as well as his heart.*

B. Women and children spared

> *Deuteronomy 20:14 But the women, and the little ones, and the cattle, and all that is in the city, even all the spoil thereof, shalt thou take unto thyself; and thou shalt eat the spoil of thine enemies, which the Lord thy God hath given thee.*

C. Enemy given opportunity to surrender

> *1 Samuel 11:2 And Nahash the Ammonite answered them, On this condition will I make a covenant with you, that I may thrust out all your right eyes, and lay it for a reproach upon all Israel.*

> *v.3 And the elders of Jabesh said unto him, Give us seven days' respite, that we may send messengers unto all the coasts of Israel: and then, if there be no man to save us, we will come out to thee.*

> *1 Samuel 30:1 And it came to pass, when David and his men were come to Ziklag on the third day, that the Amalekites had invaded the south, and Ziklag, and smitten Ziklag, and burned it with fire;*

> *v.2 And had taken the women captives, that were therein: they slew not any, either great or small, but carried them away, and went on their way.*

D. Total destruction ordered for corrupting influences

> *Deuteronomy 20:16 But of the cities of these people, which the Lord thy God doth give thee for an inheritance, thou shalt save alive nothing that breatheth:*

> *v.17 But thou shalt utterly destroy them; namely, the Hittites, and the Amorites, the Canaanites, and the Perizzites, the Hivites, and the Jebusites; as the Lord thy God hath commanded thee:*

> *v.18 That they teach you not to do after all their abominations, which they have done unto their gods; so should ye sin against the Lord your God.*

III. NEW TESTAMENT SOLDIERS

A. Held positions of honor

Acts 10:1   There was a certain man in Caesarea called Cornelius, a centurion of the band called the Italian band.

v.2   A devout man, and one that feared God with all his house, which gave much alms to the people, and prayed to God alway.

v.3   He saw in a vision evidently about the ninth hour of the day an angel of God coming in to him, and saying unto him, Cornelius.

v.4   And when he looked on him, he was afraid, and said, What is it, Lord? And he said unto him, Thy prayers and thine alms are come up for a memorial before God.

Acts 10:34   Then Peter opened his mouth, and said, Of a truth I perceive that God is no respecter of persons:

v.35   But in every nation he that feareth him, and worketh righteousness, is accepted with him.

2 Timothy 2:4   No man that warreth entangleth himself with the affairs of this life; that he may please him who hath chosen him to be a soldier.

B. A model for Christians

Ephesians 6:11   Put on the whole armour of God, that ye may be able to stand against the wiles of the devil.

v.12   For we wrestle not against flesh and blood, but against principalities, against powers, against the rulers of the darkness of this world, against spiritual wickedness in high places.

v.13   Wherefore take unto you the whole armour of God, that ye may be able to withstand in the evil day, and having done all, to stand.

v.14   Stand therefore, having your loins girt about with truth, and having on the breastplate of righteousness;

v.15   And your feet shod with the preparation of the gospel of peace;

v.16 Above all, taking the shield of faith, wherewith ye shall be able to quench all the fiery darts of the wicked.

v.17 And take the helmet of salvation, and the sword of the Spirit, which is the word of God.

CONCLUSION

As each letter comes into the ministry, the response — as well as the need — becomes a matter of prayer.

The Word of God truly does have the answer for every need of mankind. I encourage you to continually dig into the Word of God, mining its rich treasure.

Paul admonished Timothy to study the Scriptures, so he would never be without an answer for his faith (2 Timothy 2:15).

John instructs us that the Holy Spirit will lead us into all truth (John 16:13).

James tells us if we lack wisdom to ask God for it (James 1:5).

As you continue in your quest for truth, I believe this study will prove its value. Solomon, the wisest man who ever lived, said that wisdom would give us life and defend us. (Ecclesiastes 7:12). Having wisdom is better than any strength and better than any weapon (Ecclesiastes 9:16,18).

The truth *that you know* is the truth that will set you free (John 8:32). The truth of the Word of God will deliver you from everything that holds you back.

As you give time and attention to the study of the Bible, you will move forward into the things of God with new freedom, new understanding and new insight.

BIBLIOGRAPHY

Dake, Finis Jennings. *Dake's Annotated Reference Bible*. Lawrenceville: Dake Bible Sales, Inc., 1963.

Eastman, Dick. *The Hour that Changes the World*. Grand Rapids: Baker Book House Company, 1978.

Kotal, Joseph A. *The Fruit of the Spirit*. Melbourne: Harbour House Publishers of Fine Books, 1989.

Nelson, P.C. *Bible Doctrines*. Springfield: Gospel Publishing House, 1948.

Prater, Arnold. *You Can Pray As You Ought*. Nashville: Thomas Nelson Inc., Publishers, 1977.

Smith, Dr. William. *Smith's Bible Dictionary*. Philadelphia: A.J. Holman Company, n.d.

Strong, James. *Strong's Exhaustive Concordance*. Nashville: Crusade Bible Publishers, Inc., n.d.

Barclay, William. *The Letters to the Galatians and Ephesians*. Philadelphia: The Westminster Press, 1976.

Willmington, H.L. *The King is Coming*. Wheaton: Tyndale House Publishers, 1973.

Revival is *Falling in Love c̄ Jesus

True Repentance*

Whole Body

Relationship c̄ Jesus Christ.

Let God be God. Anointing.

5 Fold Ministry

Evangelism.

Revival = Inside of you. Not a physical thing.